EDUCATION MATTERS

General Editor: Ted Wragg

THE EDUCATION OF GIRLS

BOOKS IN THIS SERIES

Adult Education *by Michael D. Stephens*

The Education of Girls *by Jane French*

Higher Education *by Donald Bligh*

Learning in Primary Schools *by Andrew Pollard*

Managing Finance in Schools *by Tim Blanchard, Bob Lovell and Nick Ville*

The New Curriculum *by Richard Pring*

Schools and Parents *by John Partington and Ted Wragg*

Secondary Education *by Maureen O'Connor*

Testing and Assessment *by Charles Desforges*

Vocational Education and Training *by Patrick Ainley*

THE EDUCATION OF GIRLS

A HANDBOOK
FOR PARENTS

Jane French

CASSELL

Cassell Educational Limited
Villiers House
41/47 Strand
London WC2N 5JE
England

First published 1990

British Library Cataloguing in Publication Data
French, Jane
  The education of girls : a handbook for parents. –
  (Education matters).
  1. Great Britain. Girls. Education
  I. Title II. Series
  376.941

ISBN 0–304–32258–X (hardback)
       0–304–32278–4 (paperback)

Phototypeset by Input Typesetting Ltd, London

Printed and bound in Great Britain by
Biddles Ltd, Guildford and King's Lynn

CONTENTS

FOREWORD

Professor E. C. Wragg, Exeter University

During the 1980s a succession of Education Acts changed considerably the nature of schools and their relationships with the outside world. Parents were given more rights and responsibilities, including the opportunity to serve on the governing body of their child's school. The 1988 Education Reform Act in particular, by introducing for the first time a National Curriculum, the testing of children at the ages of 7, 11, 14 and 16, local management, including financial responsibility and the creation of new types of school, was a radical break with the past. Furthermore the disappearance of millions of jobs, along with other changes in our society, led to reforms not only of schools, but also of further and higher education.

In the wake of such rapid and substantial changes it was not just parents and lay people, but also teachers and other professionals working in education, who found themselves struggling to keep up with what these many changes meant and how to get the best out of them. The *Education Matters* series addresses directly the major topics of reform, such as the new curriculum, testing and assessment, the role of parents and the handling of school finances, considering their effects on primary, secondary, further and higher education, and also the continuing education of adults.

The aim of the series is to present information about the challenges facing education in the remainder of the twentieth century in an authoritative but readable form. The books in the series, therefore, are of particular interest to parents, governors and all those concerned with education, but are written in such a way as to give an overview to students, experienced teachers and other professionals who work in the field.

Each book gives an account of the relevant legislation and background, but, more importantly, stresses practical implications of change with specific examples of what is being or can be done to make reforms work effectively. The authors are not only authorities in their field, but also have direct experience of the matters they write about. That is why the *Education Matters* series makes an important contribution to both debate and practice.

INTRODUCTION

Over the past twenty years, attitudes towards girls and their education have changed. Although most girls will still grow up to become wives and mothers, this is by no means all that they will do, or expect to do, with their lives. The arrival on the scene of reliable forms of contraception, higher than ever levels of educational achievement, and a gradually improving sense of self-confidence among the female population mean that girls and their parents have come to expect far more of themselves, of their schools and of their teachers than was the case a generation or so ago.

Research carried out over the same period of time has thrown up some intriguing findings. We have become more aware, for example, of subtle differences in the ways that we, as adults, react to girls and boys, of the ways in which teachers respond differently to the two sexes, of differences in the behaviour of the children themselves. And some, at least, of these differences in reaction and behaviour affect both the developing child's sense of self-worth, and the experience of education itself.

My aim in the following chapters has been to select and present what I see as the important issues and debates in a readable form, in the hope that more parents will become aware of the particular needs of their daughters, and of the likely problems and pitfalls. On a more positive note, I hope that they will be helped towards informed choices and courses of action; so that they know what to ask of teachers and schools, and how best to offer support from home, both in the early years and as their daughters proceed through the education system.

Jane French
March 1990

1

Chapter 1

BACKGROUND STORY

Education for girls – a potted history

The education of girls has had something of a chequered past, slipping in and out of the public eye and interest as expectations have changed and progress has been fought for and won. Until the nineteenth century, when organised campaigning really began to gain momentum, provision was very haphazard – a position matched by the achievements of the girls themselves. A fortunate few were able to scale the heights of scholarship. But any survey of the remaining female population would have shown an enormous range of attainment, from those who could sing, dance and paint very prettily (and – for let us not denigrate their achievements – sometimes very well), to those with a sound competence in the basics, and finally to those who were totally illiterate and had had no formal education at all.

By the early nineteenth century, which is where the modern story really begins, definite patterns had emerged. Anyone who is familiar with the lives and works of such well-known figures as Jane Austen or the Brontë sisters will know that, by this time, the daughters of wealthy landowning or, increasingly, industrialist or business families used mainly to learn at home, usually from a governess. Sometimes they would share a tutor with their brothers, until the boys went away, as was customary, to one of the great public schools.

For those toward the middle-class position on the social scale – including, like the Brontës, the daughters of clergymen – there might be a charity school run by a religious foundation, or instruction at home from parents or the local curate, or attendance at a young ladies' college or seminary. But school fees were expensive. The biographer Josephine Kamm quotes one early Victorian mamma as saying that no mother 'of good position' would have dreamed of sending her daughters to a day school – 'these were only for the lower classes'. So, as Kamm points out, where money was limited and keeping up appearances mattered,

a daughter's prospects would be cheerfully sacrificed to pay for an expensive education for the sons: and while there were excellent day schools for boys, for the daughters of the middle- and upper-classes there were none.

J. Kamm, *How Different from Us*, p. 10

For those at the bottom of the social heap, who, it must be remembered, represented the majority, there might be a charity school, often attached to some form of local craft or industry, or a once-a-week Sunday school. Or, depending upon where they lived, a school based upon the monitorial systems devised by Joseph Lancaster and by Andrew Bell, or founded by one of the great Victorian philanthropists. All types of school for children of this stratum were designed to provide instruction in the basics of reading, writing, arithmetic, and general and religious knowledge. And in all there was a strong emphasis on social order; a concern with keeping the children of the poor off the streets and out of the way of respectable people. It is a theme which can be traced in numerous period-piece stories, poems and songs, often using biblical texts as their base.

This form of basic education was founded, most social historians now agree, upon a genuine fear of the masses; of what might happen if dissatisfactions were widely and openly expressed, and the poor began, *en masse*, to question the structure of a society which permitted such vast discrepancies in wealth, position and power between rich and poor. With the example of the French Revolution of 1789 well within living memory in early Victorian Britain, this attitude is understandable.

But as the nineteenth century progressed, and the Industrial Revolution took firm hold, the great manufacturing towns and cities also developed – with their attendant social problems. Great and increasing populations of the poor became concentrated in particular urban areas, giving rise to renewed anxiety on the part of those who predicted wide-scale revolt, and to anger among influential philanthropists and social reformers who found the conditions in which the labouring poor were forced to exist an affront to civilised society. Within this context of industrial development, population growth and social concern, the demand for a system of state education, free and available to all began to grow. The debate was to be long-winded, heated and sometimes acrimonious. Those who opposed it were terrified that 'a little learning would be a dangerous thing'; education might lead the poor to question the position in life which, they were told, God had ordained. And as late as the 1860s, there was a general feeling that education for girls in particular was socially and morally dubious as well as being a waste of time. In the Report of the Commissioners to the Schools' Inquiry Commission in 1868, James Bryce observed:

although the world has now existed for several thousand years (*sic*), the notion that women have minds as cultivable and worth cultivating as men's minds is still regarded by the ordinary British parent as an offensive, not to say a revolutionary, paradox.

But despite the opposition, progress was inevitable. Over the course of a series of Acts dating from 1836 and continuing into the present century, education for both girls and boys became free and compulsory. And in the nineteenth century there were many milestones in the progression of girls and women toward greater educational rights, with outstanding campaigning figures such as Emily Davies, Dorothea Beale, founder of Cheltenham Ladies' College, and Frances Mary Buss, founder of the North London Collegiate School, standing as examples of their achievements. At the end of the First World War in 1918, women over the age of 30 were given the vote. Ten years later, in 1928, this right was extended to women over the age of 21 – the final pinnacle for those involved in what had been a bitter and violent struggle.

Steady progress was made during the inter-war years, with the foundation of many of the girls' day schools, and a steady rise in the numbers of girls going on to higher education. But with the benefit of hindsight, it is also possible to detect a growing mood of complacency, on the part of politicians and the general public at least, by the late 1940s. Perhaps it was a sense of victory and achievement at having gained the vote, together with the experience of two world wars which led to a general acceptance of continuing, niggling injustices and anomalies.

These included differing entry requirements for women and men at Oxford and Cambridge, or quota systems in the medical profession, so that the number of young women qualifying as doctors was strictly limited. But the most widespread injustice, which has affected the largest number of children, was the setting of a higher pass mark for girls than for boys in the eleven-plus examination. Because of this practice, girls who actually gained higher marks than boys were denied a grammar school education. (This is, of course, not to enter into the wider argument concerning the rights and wrongs of any form of selection at eleven-plus.) These sorts of widespread and, until recently, largely unchallenged practices effectively handicapped thousands of bright and able girls and young women, and squandered their intellectual talents.

It took the upheaval of attitudes which came about in the 1960s before women began loudly and persistently to question deep-seated assumptions, and to put the education of girls and women firmly back on the educational and political agenda. It has remained there for the past twenty years.

The legacy of the 1960s has now itself been called into question. But while, with hindsight, the excesses of that period may now seem absurd, the idealism naïve, there is a residue of ideas whose currency has been modified but not altogether diminished by the passage of time. From the point of view of women in particular, the 1960s provided a stepping-stone to areas of employment where few or no women have gone before, raised expectations, and, perhaps most important of all, improved women's sense of self-worth.

5

Life after marriage

Arguably, the single most significant shift in attitudes concerned the position of women after marriage and children. Before the 1960s, it was generally assumed that mothers stayed at home. Of course, many ordinary, working-class women in fact combined work in the mill, factory or shop with motherhood. But the aspiration, so graphically and innocently portrayed in all those 1950s and 1960s television advertisements, was home-centred; the dream was that of a husband who earned enough to support the whole family, so that the wife didn't have to work but was instead cocooned in cosy domesticity. For the middle-class woman too, the vision of hearth and home loomed large. There was an assumption of a 'good' marriage to a business or professional man, a pleasant home with all mod. cons and another woman to clean it; even, perhaps, a little runabout car. And afterwards, when the children were grown, charitable works or a suitable part-time job.

These aspirations linger on. For working-class women in particular, choices have always been more restricted and the views of their educated, emancipated sisters a few rungs up the social scale have done comparatively little to broaden the canvas or change traditional patterns. And given the conditions in which most women work, with low pay and poor prospects, it has never surprised me that many long for the relative autonomy and comfort of their own homes. But for a sizeable and growing minority, things have changed. First, marriage and motherhood is no longer seen as the only, lifelong option, and nor need it signal the end of a promising career. Second, and just as important, it is no longer seen, and should no longer be seen, as a lowly option for those who choose it.

Education and employment

Since the 1960s, patterns of employment have also changed. The economic recession of the early 1980s and the decline in the traditional manufacturing and heavy industries created areas of high unemployment and increased levels of comparative poverty. Faith in education as a means of climbing up the social ladder was shaken, for it was no longer possible to assure children that their prospects would be good if they would only buckle down and work. Employers who used to ask for little in the way of paper qualifications raised their standards well beyond the reach of many average and below average young people. In some cases, they now need A levels where O levels used to be enough, a degree where, in the past, A levels were quite sufficient. But because most parents have little to pass on to their children in the way of money, education is still a major priority: a benefit which can be provided to guard, as well as possible, against an uncertain future.

In the case of girls, there is a growing awareness, especially among parents who are well educated themselves, that good schooling is now, more than ever, essential. Girls face particular problems in later life which can be cushioned, if not disposed of altogether, by the security of sound academic, practical or vocational qualifications.

Divorce and its implications for women

It is well known that the divorce rate has soared in the past 20 or 30 years. In 1961, 25,000 decrees absolute were granted in England and Wales. By 1985, the figure was running at 160,000. Obviously, this is a matter of great concern for all involved either in loveless partnership or family life, or in the upset and upheaval of marriage break-up. Thinking particularly, in the context of this book, of the difficulties faced by mothers with dependent children, it is quite clear that many such women face financial ruin if their relationships with men collapse. This is, despite the publicity heaped upon the occasional well-known man handing out enormous alimony payments to an embittered ex-wife, the reality for countless ordinary people. For the non-earning wife with young children, divorce or widowhood can mean dependence on social security payments and loss of house. Just as important to her psychological well-being, and affecting divorced men as well as women, it can also lead to loss of status in the community. And this is not to mention the stress of helping children come to terms with the new situation.

With mounting public concern over the high divorce rate and its effect on families, couples may begin to take the responsibilities of parenthood more seriously. Men – for more women than men sue for divorce – may become better husbands. The divorce rate may bottom out. But the ability of a woman to look after herself, to earn sufficient money so that, if the worst happens, she is left with a means of support for herself and her children is still of obvious and continuing importance. And given that the majority of women do not have inherited wealth or investment income to provide them with a living, education is still the established and favoured route to long-term security.

Women and employment

Bearing in mind the question of divorce and its devastating effects on family life, it is worth thinking about employment in more detail. For although some 70–80 per cent of women with school-age children are in work, they continue to be concentrated in the low-paid service occupations (such as shop work, hairdressing or catering), often with little in the way of promotion prospects, job security or benefits such as pension funds. In the event of divorce or bereavement, such women face greater difficulties than women in business or the professions, with little earning power and insufficient funds to pay for child care while they are at work.

In cases where the marriage survives (two out of every three marriages can be counted as successful in the sense that they do not end in divorce), few women can look forward to earning as much as or more than their husbands. Since 1975, women have earned around 70–75 per cent of what men can expect to earn.

Obviously, the question of low earnings and poor prospects is not a problem which can be solved by education alone. It calls for profound economic and social changes which, realistically, are unlikely to take place in the foreseeable future. But what we, as parents, teachers or generally concerned individuals *can* do is to make sure that girls and their parents are aware of these issues; that in the world as it is, and not, perhaps, as we would like it to be, women fare badly in the world of work. By facing what is a stark fact of life within the context of our existing economic system, girls and their parents can take steps to provide for the future by using the resources available to them.

I do not mean to imply here that all young women could benefit from education by entering the high-earning professions or starting their own businesses. What is too often forgotten in the so-called enterprise culture is that most people are not particularly bright or enterprising. By inclination and ability, they are employees rather than entrepreneurs: average members of the population who do not want to take on board the responsibilities of running a business, or who are not academically able to enter the élite world of the highly educated. But it remains the case that more women than men fail to discover or to make the best of their talents or themselves, settling too readily for modest expectations and mediocrity.

Traditional family relationships

Many girls and young women look to marriage as a pot of gold at the rainbow's end. Throughout the teenage years, they immerse themselves in the romantic visions churned out by the magazine industry, lapping up the myriad tips on how to be slim, pretty and attractive to men. Then having ensnared their man, there is the wedding, and a whole barrage of advice on how to be a beautiful bride. Somehow, in the midst of the preparations and homemaking, the marriage as opposed to the wedding itself slips into the background. To do them justice, the bridal magazines do tackle topics such as managing the housework, and the importance of keeping up job, interests and friends after marriage. But a special sort of maturity is needed to foresee the importance and the practical implications of these issues. So, for a great many young women, marriage is a beautiful dream; an event rather than a continuing state, which they have probably anticipated for years.

With luck, the early years of marriage can be a period of fulfilment and comparative prosperity, although decisions which could affect the wife for years to come may be in the balance. What should be done, for example, if she is offered promotion or a job in another town? But it is with motherhood that the most profound changes occur.

Although more and more women nowadays take maternity leave (if they are entitled to it), most mothers in fact give up work on the birth of their first child. For many of them it is a rewarding and fulfilling experience, and there is great pleasure to be had in sharing in the growth and development of children. So to me, it is easy to see why so many women make this particular choice. I have always felt that, as an option, it has been somewhat undervalued and even sneered at by certain sections of the Women's Movement. There is surely nothing whatsoever wrong with anybody concentrating her energies on being a wife and mother rather than a career woman – if that is her informed and happy choice.

There is a lot wrong, however, with the social context in which being a housewife in late twentieth-century Britain occurs. First, a non-earning housewife is economically dependent on her husband. This is fine if the husband is fair-minded and if the marriage is regarded as a partnership with the two playing separate but equal roles. But in cases where the husband refuses to say how much he earns, squanders money or keeps his wife short of it, or if there is domestic violence, the situation is less than satisfactory. If the marriage breaks up, the wife can, as was pointed out earlier, face financial disaster on top of emotional turmoil.

Then there is a great deal of evidence to suggest that housewives, especially if they have young children and not much money, suffer a lot from stress-related conditions. The majority of people taking tranquillising drugs, for example, are young women at home with children.

This should not surprise us at all: for the first time in our history, women are often expected to take on the role of housewife and mother in social isolation. Although, as a nation, we are materially better off than ever before, and for most families the stress of not knowing where the next meal is coming from has disappeared, new forms of stress have been generated by progress and prosperity. Many families, for example, are now scattered all over the country, and sometimes the world, so that mothers, sisters, cousins and aunts are no longer on hand to help. Nor is there, nowadays, the army of servants who eased the burden for even the lower echelons of the middle classes before the First World War. And the housing estates where many families now live are dismally short of the sorts of resources which used to be taken for granted wherever communities grew and settled. Shops, schools, doctors' surgeries, libraries and public transport are all as absent from our meticulously designed housing developments as they are, now, in our rural villages. Little wonder that housewives get depressed!

It now seems too that children can suffer from the sort of over-intense relationships which being at home together all the time can produce. Some psychologists now believe that children actually benefit from seeing their mother rather less often! The ideal relationship is perhaps much more like the relationships mothers and children used to have in days gone by – when the extended family of grandparents, aunts and uncles and so on played a more important part in a child's upbringing, and where children were allowed more freedom to play with brothers, sisters and friends outside the home. In other words, towards the one-to-many instead of the one-to-one end of an imaginary relationship spectrum.

From the point of view of the mother, the housewife role can also lead to a loss of self-esteem. In a society where success is defined in terms of earnings, where what people *are* is so much bound up with what they *do*, it is small wonder that the apologetic phrase 'just a housewife' is still so frequently heard.

I agree with those who argue that we should reorganise our priorities; that we should respond to the person and not the label. But the practice of categorising people by their work, and of an occupational label carrying so much social information about a person seems to me to be so ingrained as to be immutable. While hoping that in some ideal world such labelling would cease to matter, we have to realise that people living in the real world have to cope, every day, with the reactions of other people to them. And the taken-for-granted view is, of course, that being a housewife is boring; that the housewife is obsessed with trivia, from the colour of her curtains to the astonishing properties of her neighbour's new cooker. It is seen as boring, too, to speak about one's children. There is an unspoken rule which allows a man to run through all the doings at the office in meticulous detail, but which discourages a woman from recounting her child's latest sayings or escapades. So a housewife tends to be treated, and may come to see herself, as uninteresting – a nonentity with nothing of worth to offer.

How can education help?

It is always a mistake to assume that education can solve all our social and political problems, even if we can all agree as to what exactly they are! But even as one of nature's pessimists, I still believe that it has a positive role to play.

First of all, educational qualifications do still provide a passport to the job market. Although a university degree can no longer be regarded as a ticket to privilege, it undoubtedly helps. The better qualified person – and this applies to every field I can think of – can still command the better wage or salary, the better working conditions and prospects, the more comfortable life-style.

But education has more than a mere use value. It is also a civilising and enriching influence which changes people's perceptions of the world around them, of their own situation in time and place. This is a value which cannot be quantified, but which should never be underestimated in our educational reckonings – perhaps especially where women and girls are concerned. As I shall argue throughout this book, psychological well-being is as important as or more important than material prosperity.

Until very recently, girls did not do nearly so well out of the education system as boys. My own mother must be one among many who, in the 1940s and because of their sex, were denied a grammar school education. These attitudes live on. Only recently, a friend revealed to me that she would be willing to pay for the education of her son but not her daughter on the grounds that, like it or not, a boy's education was more important than that of a girl.

In this book, I hope to convince people who perhaps sympathise with that point of view that the education of their daughter is every bit as important as that of their son. That in the way they go about being a parent to their daughter, in choosing a school, in what they do and what they do not encourage, they are either extending or foreclosing on her options far into adult life.

For the growing band of the already converted, I will explain some of the ways in which they can help to give girls a wider choice; in which they can use the education system instead of being intimidated by it. In the chapters which follow, I discuss a number of issues arising from the pre-school years through to young adulthood. I summarise important research findings which have appeared within the professional, academic literature over the past twenty years, but which are largely inaccessible to the majority of people. On a practical level, I suggest ways in which parents can help their daughters, from the provision of toys and outside experiences to choosing the right school and influencing school policy.

Only when girls make full use of our schools and take up the opportunities which are opening up, when more women come forward to serve in local and national government, in professional bodies and in the Trades Union movement will the world become more responsive to the needs and capabilities of over half the population.

Chapter 2
BEGINNINGS

Boy or girl?

One of the first things a mother wants to know about her newborn baby is its sex. Girl or boy, the sex of a child affects the development of the parent–child relationship from the outset. Some hospitals provide pink or blue blankets, friends and relatives send boys' or girls' greetings cards, and sex-appropriate toys or clothes begin to appear. When our daughter was born, we were showered with cuddly toys – fluffy rabbits, chubby teddies and hideous creatures, of no known species, with luminous eyes! Our son received only a handful, and two of those were bought by us! Instead, he was given mobiles, small wooden toys and useful things like spoon sets, bibs, beakers and clothes.

But buying girls' toys or boys' toys, providing girls' clothes or boys' clothes represent only the more obvious ways in which we treat the sexes differently. Researchers who have studied parents with their young children have noticed other, more subtle, but potentially important differences. One general tendency is for parents to see little girls as in need of a greater degree of protection, as more fragile and vulnerable, and to treat them accordingly. In fact, little girls are *less* vulnerable to both disease and birth defects, and more likely to survive severe illness. Perhaps the fact that baby girls are, on average, slightly smaller than baby boys makes them appear more fragile. But there is more to it than that. Fragility is also in the eye of the beholder.

Spot the difference

In one intriguing and widely reported experiment by C. Smith and B. Lloyd ('Maternal Behaviour and Perceived Sex of Infant'), a 6-month-old baby was dressed as a little girl, given a girl's name and handed to adults, ostensibly to see how 'she' reacted to being handled by strangers. The same baby was then dressed as a boy, given a boy's name, and a second group of adults was asked to handle 'him'. The results were interesting. If the adults thought they were playing with a girl, they treated large motor movements as a sign of distress, hugging the baby and cuddling 'her' to them. Similar movements on the part of a 'boy' were interpreted as playful; the adults bounced the baby on their knees and tried to jolly 'him' along. By responding differently to the same sort of behaviour in boys and girls, parents and other adults actively, although perhaps unknowingly, encourage the sexes to behave differently. Variations on this experiment are reported elsewhere (see, for example, L. R. Walum, *The Dynamics of Sex and Gender*), and reach essentially similar conclusions.

In other ways too, we see what we want to see. I vividly remember one little boy, of about 8 or 9 months, who was brought to play at our house when my daughter was a baby. He sat on the carpet, playing very contentedly with a doll, poking its eyes, pulling its hair and generally enjoying himself as babies do. This went on for several minutes, during which his mother monitored him, but said not a word about the doll. A few moments later, he picked up a toy car. The mother immediately drew attention to it, exclaiming 'Oh, he loves cars, don't you?' and got down on the floor to play with him. It was as though the doll could be tolerated, whereas the car was positively to be encouraged.

'Boys cry more' – or do they?

Adults also use the sex of a baby as an explanation for behaviour which they find puzzling. Excessive crying, for example, is often put down to the fact that a baby is male – 'boys cry more'. There is no reliable basis for this observation in Britain at least, where studies of newborns have shown the sexes to cry equally. But as Sara Delamont in her book *Sex Roles and the School* explains, it was discovered some years ago that boys in the USA *did* cry more than girls, and also appeared to thrash about more with their arms and legs. At

15

first, this was put down, simply, to their sex, and taken as confirmation that boys are more active and aggressive than girls. Then researchers noticed that it was only boys from the USA who seemed to cry a lot – their British counterparts were apparently more contented. The explanation for the discrepancy was that all the US boys had been circumcised and were suffering varying degrees of post-operative pain.

Building on the differences

But having made the point that our expectations colour our perceptions, I should add that I am by no means of the school of thought which dismisses biologically-based differences between the sexes. I do not subscribe to the view that all the sex-related discrepancies we see in the behaviour of adult men and women are due to differences in upbringing rather than biology. Despite the 'failure' of the US experiment cited in the previous section, it is well established, for example, that males are generally more aggressive than females (E. E. Maccoby and C. N. Jacklin, *The Psychology of Sex Differences*). But the experience of growing up is to exaggerate and to develop the differences that do exist. And as we shall see in this and the following chapters, the cumulative effect of years of this type of response from adults, in both the home and in pre-school organisations such as play groups and nurseries, is to amplify the differences. Our attitudes, the things that we choose to draw attention to, and those that we choose to ignore, have lasting consequences. And, for girls especially, they can be deleterious in both social and educational terms.

Sex and gender

There are those who may be forgiven for wondering why on earth it matters if we treat boys and girls differently; especially if there are differences between them. Surely it is only natural and to be expected?

This point of view gains further support from the fact that there is no society in the world where boys and girls, men and women are treated in exactly the same way. But it is important to remember that each society has its own, slightly different, ideas as to what males and females should be like, how they should look, act, dress – what sort of people they should be. Hence the distinction very often made by anthropologists and sociologists between *biological sex*, which is given, and *social gender*, which is learned.

Although certain of her findings have recently been contested (D. Freeman, *Margaret Mead and Samoa*), the work of the anthropologist Margaret Mead has always seemed to turn many of our assumptions regarding masculinity and femininity on their heads. She, and scholars who came after, described tribes where it is thought right, proper and natural for women to be aggressive and men passive, where boys chatter about trivia while girls discuss matters of more importance, where women rather than men are thought to be built for heavy work such as lifting and carrying (M. Mead, *Male and Female*; A. Oakley, *Sex, Gender and Society*). Within the industrialised world, the Soviets consider engineering to be a perfectly proper job for a woman, while in Britain it is still a predominantly male occupation. In Germany, boys apparently experience less difficulty in learning to read than girls (C. A. Dwyer, 'Sex Differences in Reading'), while the reverse is true in Britain. Commonsense thinking in both nations is that this is caused by biological sex differences! And, of course, opinions change over time. It is only a century ago that the study of mathematics and science was thought to impair a woman's ability to have children!

It can therefore be limiting to both sexes (although here we are concerned specifically with the female sex) to think of differences as natural and fixed. What counts as natural varies over time and from place to place. There are, and will probably always be, some biologically based differences in temperament between the average man and the average woman. But in an advanced, mechanised society such as our own, biological sex matters less and less in the world of education, and in the occupational world. Girls have shown themselves to be more than the equals of boys in terms of numbers of public examination passes, a fact which would have astounded our ancestors of little over a century ago. And as heavy industry has declined, and technology has advanced, physical strength in the workplace has become less necessary. At the same time, women have become less tied to the biological function of bearing children. Reliable forms of contraception and improved health care facilities mean that we do not have to have large numbers of children, and that the children that we do have are more likely to survive.

Yet too often, still, in both obvious and more subtle ways, we set girls on the path to domesticity, and boys out into the world. We forget that, fulfilling though the roles of wife and mother may be, the time when a woman is at home with small children represents a comparatively short chunk of her adult life. Before that time, she will need to work, she may continue to work when her children are small, and she will almost certainly work again when they have gone to school.

This does not mean that work is or ought to be seen, yuppie-fashion, as the mainspring of existence. Comparatively few people in fact enjoy the privilege of job satisfaction or career development. For the majority, employment is a means to an end, and nothing more. There are too, nowadays, large numbers of well-educated people, perhaps the majority of whom are women, who are prevented by changing patterns of employment or family commitments from reaching the dizzy heights of the career ladder. The need to find emotional and psychological satisfaction outside the environment of paid employment remains. But as parents, we have to look to the future on behalf of our daughters, to enable them to make the best of the opportunities that school can provide, both for the sake of their career prospects, and their psychological well-being. We have to try to make them inwardly confident, so that they are not discouraged by people who say that this or that is 'not for girls'. We have to make them feel that they have some measure of control over their future, that girls, as well as boys, matter. And setting this trend in motion begins with confidence-building in infancy, and continues throughout the childhood years.

The home environment

It is generally acknowledged that a child's education begins in the home. Countless sociological and educational studies have documented the influence of family and surrounding community in shaping attitudes, and furnishing the child with an orientation to both education and life in general. But few people have provided any detailed accounts of sex-role socialisation in the home: that is, the ways in which very young children learn to behave appropriately as little girls or boys.

This is partly due to problems of access: it would be difficult to mount the sort of long-term, intensive, fly-on-the-wall-type study which would yield the depth of information needed. And there is also the ethical question of how much the people under study are told of the investigation and its purpose. Sociologists are bound by their professional associations to disclose the nature of research interests. But in so doing, they unavoidably prejudice the naturalness of subjects' behaviour. If parents know, for example, that their attitudes to and their practice in the upbringing of girls and boys are under study, particular pressures are brought to bear. They may feel constrained to behave more liberally than is normally the case, or to revert to a more strict observance of traditional patterns than usual. In any case, the normal, everyday behaviour which the researcher aims to capture is likely to prove elusive.

For these reasons, the knowledge that we have about sex-role socialisation is often gleaned from a whole range of sources; sometimes, incidentally, from studies whose primary focus was another, quite different, issue. So, in the sections that follow, I have drawn on a variety of material from academic studies, from a diary account of a little girl's earliest years, and from my own observations.

Get ready to play – girls and their clothes

Next time you go to your local park, have a close look at the girls and boys playing there. It is still sadly commonplace to see little boys dressed in scruffy play clothes swarming all over the swings, slides and climbing frames, and little girls dressed in restrictive and over-fussy garments, which must not be dirtied or which actually prevent them from swinging, climbing or scrambling. I have seen female babies and toddlers, whose natural inclinations lead them to crawl and explore, decked out like dolls in cumbersome dresses, frilly knickers and patent leather shoes, not to mention the ubiquitous white socks! And I have seen older girls in tight skirts and mini court shoes, which constrain free movement and are also potentially dangerous.

Of course, there is a place for smart, pretty and fashionable clothes, and as they grow older, girls (and boys!) crave, and plead, for the latest styles. But while they are young, it surely behoves all parents to invest in a couple of sets of play clothes.

Writing in 1980, Sara Delamont pointed out discrepancies in the sorts of play clothes stocked by some of our major retail stores. Referring to the Mothercare, UK catalogues for summer and winter 1978, she discovered that the clothes on offer were sharply sex-differentiated once babyhood was left behind, and that only boys were shown in track suits. As she put it, 'if ever there was a garment designed for activity, and suitable for both sexes, it is the track suit. Adult women athletes wear them, but not the children in the Mothercare books' (S. Delamont, *Sex Roles and the School*, p. 14). Surprisingly, as we enter the last decade of the twentieth century, there are still discrepancies in the range of play clothes available for boys and for girls. In their 1989 autumn/winter catalogue, for example, Mothercare, UK (still one of the largest retail outlets for children's clothes) offers seven categories of dress under the heading 'Colourful fashion ideas for younger children up to 6 years':

> Girls' separates
> Girls' dresses
> Girls' outerwear
>
>
> Boys' separates
> Boys' suits
> Boys' leisure
> Boys' outerwear

There is no category for girls which corresponds to 'Boys' leisure', and of course it is this category which contains the four all-purpose jogging suits, two American football shirts, and one set (choice of colours!) of American football jogging pants. So although a more restricted range of similar, loose, leisure garments is available for girls, it is found under 'Girls' separates'. A subtle difference in expectation perhaps, but it is the combination of a range of such subtle differences in our attitudes towards boys and girls which makes up their everyday reality: a reality where the most basic childhood requirements seem to be differentiated by sex.

My own approach to this problem has always been to buy ultra-cheap (sometimes boys') play clothes from bargain stores and to avoid the designer-type jeans and co-ordinated track suits which, it seems to me, are for the sporty look rather than the grubby actuality. A couple of cheap pairs of shorts and T-shirts, and perhaps a track suit allow little girls the freedom to climb, dig, play with water, and get themselves muddy without making parents tense at the prospect of expensive clothing being ruined. And, importantly, in allowing girls the sort of freedom which is so taken for granted by boys, also provides opportunities for them to gain a sense of control over the physical environment.

Parental attitudes

Suitable clothing is one prerequisite for exploring and discovering your own strengths and weaknesses. Another is the attitude of parents. While you are 'people-watching' at the park, try to sneak a close look at how mothers and fathers play with their young sons and daughters. Obviously, there are always exceptions, but to my eyes (and perhaps I am biased!) mothers tend either to hover protectively, issuing 'don't fall's and 'hold tight's at regular intervals, or, especially with older children, simply to sit and watch. Fathers seem to become more involved in playing with both sexes and, certainly with boys, to encourage them to extend and develop their existing abilities. A father will urge a small boy to 'have a go' on playground apparatus, ready to catch him if he falls.

Parents, and particularly fathers, are acutely aware, after all, that a boy must not be seen to be 'soft'; so it is important to develop a son's self-confidence, motor control and spirit of adventure.

Little girls are not under quite the same pressure. It is far more acceptable for a girl to be apprehensive when it comes to climbing, swinging or jumping than for a boy. So it is not altogether surprising to find that although some fathers do take the trouble to encourage their daughters and enlarge upon their existing skills, others are content to stay within the bounds set by either the nature of the equipment or their daughters' current limitations. Thus we see fathers catching their daughters at the bottom of the slide, or pushing them on the swings while the boys go on the assault course or play on the climbing frame.

Few of us would like to see fathers using the over-hearty and occasionally cruel tactics that some of them see fit to inflict upon their sons with their daughters as well. But in a loving context and with a bit of common sense, they can do a lot to develop the physical abilities and the self-confidence of girls as well as boys.

I feel strongly that mothers too should learn to play with their daughters. Too often, children regard Dad as the jolly, indulgent parent and Mum as the one who is forever busy, tired, or putting paid to the fun and games. This is partly because fathers have traditionally worked outside the home and found it easier to operate with a boundary between home and work. For mothers, whether they work outside the home or not, the boundaries are not so clearly defined. Children represent both a joy and a 24-hour responsibility, and we continue to set ourselves impossible targets. It is generally mothers who feel under pressure to keep the house in *Ideal Home* order, who feel guilty at the dirty floor, pile of unwashed dishes or heap of ironing forever lurking in the background. And, sadly, it is often women who perpetuate the attitude that because a husband has been out at work, this somehow absolves him from all responsibility for household tasks once he gets home!

It is important to keep housework in perspective; to make a distinction, perhaps, between the roles of housewife and mother, and decide which is the more important of the two. Houses don't derive positive joy, pleasure and benefit from being the centre of our attention – children thrive on it. Of course it is satisfying to have a well-appointed, well-run and sparkling house, but there are more important priorities. A house which suffers a few years' neglect while the children are small can be given a face-lift later. Childhood is short and it is not repeatable. If we miss happy, relaxed times with our daughters (and, of course, our sons), doing pleasurable things together, we can never make up those times.

Toys

Toys represent one of the means by which young children learn. There is a sense, in fact, in which play is their work. But the toys we provide, and the experiences which they generate, are very often different for girls and boys. Nowadays, there are a great many unisex toys, but there are still discrepancies in what we buy for boys and girls, and in what they play with. We tend to give little girls the sorts of toys around which they can weave fantasies, use their powers of invention, and pretend. In their early years, we provide dressing-up clothes, dolls, little figures such as Playmobiles, tea sets and prams. Little girls act out games of mummies and daddies, school, tea parties, nurses. Of course, little boys play and enjoy fantasy games too. But they also seem to be provided with opportunities for a variety of further experiences. Although, in theory, they are unisex toys, boys are more likely to be given construction games such as Duplo, Lego, or, later, Meccano or its equivalents. They are also, and crucially, more likely actually to be encouraged to play with them, to have their play elaborated and extended by their parents.

The difference, even though it is of degree rather than in kind, is, I think, important. Little boys, through their play, gradually assume a sense of control over their world. The Manchester-based Girls into Science and Technology (GIST) project in the early 1980s reported that by the time they reach secondary school, boys are more confident about their abilities in subjects such as physics, even though tests show that at this age, there is no difference in actual ability. Quite simply, boys have had more practice at manipulating and observing objects, and feel more confident about it than girls. As a result, some secondary schools have experimented by providing opportunities for their first-year girls to play with the construction toys with which they should have been provided in the early years.

All little girls from the toddler stage onwards should have access to jigsaws, bricks and blocks, and shape-sorting games. They should be helped and encouraged to play with these toys, with one or other parent talking to them about the various things which can be done. Tower building (and knocking down!), sorting and examining shapes, manipulating shapes, so that they fit through spaces designed for them, are all important activities. Simple jigsaws teach children to revolve pieces so that they fit, to begin to imagine what they would look like if they were turned the other way round.

As they grow older and their manipulative skills develop, Duplo and, later, Lego are excellent. The possibilities for building, and for fantasy play, are endless. But it is essential that one or other parent sits down with their daughter to play with them. So many of the mothers with whom I discussed these ideas when preparing this book told me that their daughters simply don't like Lego or similar toys. I am sure that in many cases this is because construction toys were not an automatic choice for a daughter, the mothers communicated no enthusiasm for them, and, in the formative early years, the girls' interest was not developed – if they didn't like it, nobody bothered to persevere.

Now, nobody can guarantee that because a little girl plays with Lego or Meccano when she is small she is going to like physics or technology when she is older. The best that can be said is that it may help; that it may ease the way ahead instead of creating obstacles. This in itself is worth doing, just as it is important for girls to see their mothers becoming immersed in activities and not always, as can so easily happen, preoccupied with the mundane everyday grind.

The point about toys, then, is to provide a variety. There is nothing *wrong* with the traditional girls' toys and activities, but it is important to try other things too. I feel that it is cruel to ban toys such as dolls or the latest fad toy; so often, little girls want these things because their friends have them, and it is important for their sense of self-esteem within the peer group to be able to say 'I've got one too'. And if unisex or more masculine toys are imposed, resentment is more or less guaranteed. Probably the ideal thing is to start young, before the child has any real idea about what is and is not 'for girls'. Otherwise, tact and diplomacy have to come to the fore. And if you think she is sufficiently mature to appreciate the issues, it is always possible to explain them in simple terms.

Books

There are nowadays some excellent books for children and young people. There is also some indifferent and downright bad literature about, and it is worth taking time and trouble over the sort of books you provide. Research on school reading schemes by Glenys Lobban in the mid-1970s showed that girls and women were depicted less often than boys and men, and that when they were shown, it was within a restricted range of roles. Although the sorts of criticisms which these findings generated led to publishers up-dating their schemes, there is often a time-lag between the availability of a new scheme and its purchase by a school (G. Lobban, 'Sex Roles in Reading Schemes').

As recently as 1987, I was given a set of Ladybird readers which, until then, had been in regular use in a South Yorkshire primary school. In one of these books, two young children, Peter and Jane, go to an island with their older, male, cousins. After being soaked in a storm, they make their way back to base, where the following exchange occurs:

The two big boys start a fire in the large room. They all sit round it. The rain comes down heavily outside and they can hear and see the thunder and lightning. 'It's a real storm,' says Peter. 'We must keep inside until it is all over,' says Simon.

'I can cook,' says Jane. 'Would you like me to make you some tea and get you something to eat?'

'Yes, please,' say the boys.

Simon helps Jane to get something to eat and drink. 'It doesn't take long to make tea,' she says to her cousin. . . .

. . . He opens two of the tins for Jane to get the soup ready. Then Simon opens a tin of biscuits. He lets Jane do nearly all the work because he knows she likes to do it.

Adventure on the Island (Ladybird, 1966)

Peter and Jane also feature in the revised Ladybird Key Words scheme. Although, in the updated editions, their clothes and hair styles have been modified, and Jane is certainly less wimpish and subservient than in her previous incarnation, the two children are still portrayed, albeit more subtly, in traditional terms as far as sex roles are concerned. If she is pictured on her own, Jane does *do* things, but where she is depicted with Peter, she is more often than not in the background: she spends a good deal of time watching Peter, for example, or asking his permission to play with particular toys. And of course, she is still to be seen from time to time hovering with her tea tray! One comes away from these books with the sense that Peter gets on with things, up-front, centre-stage, while Jane watches, waits, and follows.

Now one can go too far in making claims about the damaging nature of books such as these: all those of us who went to primary school in the 1960s read them, and worse, and they have hardly confined us in a sex-role strait-jacket. There is a sense in which all young children's literature and, indeed, all forms of knowledge presented for children's consumption at this early stage deal in stereotypes; in all types of learning, one begins with clear-cut examples of a general rule, and moves on to the more complex reality once the basics are mastered. Of course, with older children, these sorts of ideas can be explored and the social and historical context in which they were written discussed. And great or even good works of literature can usually stand as such even if they are sexist, racist and everything else-ist.

One can also explain to children, as young as four or five, that a particular story is 'old-fashioned', and that 'in those days' it wasn't thought proper for girls to do X, Y or Z. But parents cannot, and indeed should not, always act as censors and thought-police for their children. While many of the reading schemes, textbooks and library books now in use in schools are delightful and of high quality, some are also likely to be either overtly or subtly sexist. But children cannot be for ever protected. Staff may be aware of the problem but may feel, especially in the case of reading schemes, that the advantages of a particular scheme in actually getting children to read outweigh any disadvantages.

Parents, therefore, have an important role to play in ensuring both that they provide books in which girls feature positively, and that they take the trouble to explain how attitudes towards girls and women and what they can do have changed. There is perhaps a tendency to buy fictional books for girls, and more of the non-fiction 'how', 'why' and 'wherefore' type for the boys. It is worth watching this. As with the toys, the sensible thing must be to buy or borrow the traditional type, but also to provide books on non-traditional topics. The much-maligned Ladybird Books have an excellent (and cheap) non-fiction range, as do Usborne Publishing.

Parents must, of course, make up their own minds as to whether they want to buy books which are specifically non-sexist. With one or two exceptions, I have always found them too contrived, and preferred, again, to talk with children about why stories such as the traditional fairy tales are written as they are. Likewise, as they get older, I can see nothing wrong with the perennial girls' favourites such as *Little Women, What Katy Did*, and so on. Quite often, the female characters in these books are resourceful and vibrant people, and the attitudes of author and characters to girls and women again make good talking points. Similarly, in the pony and school stories which so many young adolescent girls seem to love, female characters do things, have adventures, cope with adversity without male assistance. Having read them, loved them, and survived to tell the tale, I do not see them as harmful, so long as other choices are provided too.

Television

Love it or hate it, television has become a central focus in the lives of many British families. The question as to whether it is good or bad for children is notoriously difficult, and cannot possibly be resolved here (but see the References section on pp. 83–6 for a selection of reading on the subject).

My own feeling, based upon the available evidence, talking with teachers, and personal observation, is that lumpen, uncritical, and prolonged TV watching is bad. At its worst, it seems to prevent people from doing other things, transforming them into second-hand consumers of other people's reality, instead of creators of their own, and seeming almost to replace relationships with friends and family. I also feel that it leads both children and adults to become obsessed with trivia: whether two soap opera characters should or should not marry, what such and such a star likes to eat for breakfast, the (often quite unreasoned) opinions of the latest teenage heart-stopper on anything from sex to global nuclear warfare. The idolatrous fawning which over-exposure to this sort of thing inspires seems to me to epitomise popular culture at its depressing worst.

There is, however, a considerable plus side. British children's television ranks among the best in the world, and does provide an enormous variety of output which can be used sensibly to educate, to inform or simply to entertain. As with so many issues involved in the upbringing and education of children, parents have to use their common sense and to strike a balance which works in their particular situation. In our family, we watch selectively. This doesn't mean that we only ever watch serious, informative programmes, or that we never just flop in front of some mindless but entertaining drivel. But it does mean that, as a general rule, we watch programmes we want to see, and when we are not watching we get on with other things.

It is also well worth making the effort to watch with one's children, and to talk about the content and style of the programmes seen. While they are young and vulnerable, I do like to have some idea of what my children are watching, I don't want them to be bombarded with advertising, nor do I particularly want them to see third-rate imported cartoons designed to boost sales of the glitzy toys that are marketed alongside them, or to become immersed in the popular, television culture, which is very much a part of children's television output nowadays.

On the specific issue of the treatment of girls by writers and producers, there is still a tendency for them to feature as peripheral characters, although the situation has improved considerably over recent years. Depending on what you watch, however (and we must not forget that many children also watch adult television), the message may still come over loud and clear that success is equated with beauty, that girls and women are largely decorative, and that they exist forever to act as supportive foils to male characters! It is up to parents to encourage their children, male and female, to watch critically and intelligently, and to foster other interests so that passive television watching does not come to replace active pursuits and hobbies.

The peer group

The period of what sociologists call 'primary socialisation' in the home and surrounding community is crucial to the developing child's sense of self. And, within this context, and depending upon the personality of the individual child, the peer group is more or less important. There are some children who seem to be quite happy to 'be themselves' regardless of what other children think, say or do. For others, the merest hint of disapproval from an admired friend is enough to change the habits of an, albeit short, lifetime!

In the early years, children tend to play around rather than with one another. At about the age of 3, sometimes earlier, sometimes later, they begin to play co-operatively. This coincides with the time when they begin to understand the nature of their sexual identity: that they are either a boy or a girl, and that their biological sex is fixed.

A diary account written by a German mother of her daughter's experiences in the first three years of life provides us with some ideas as to the influence of the peer group, and the particular ways in which it might affect girls. One of the most important observations to emerge from Marianne Grabrucker's account is that girls are taught to adapt to the needs of boys. Time and again, she recounts episodes where the antisocial behaviour of her daughter's male peers is allowed to pass unchallenged by the adults present, and her daughter is thus cast into situations in which she is ultimately the loser. While I came away thinking, somewhat irritatedly, that the mother should have intervened on far more occasions than she did, and that the child was unusually observant in matters relating to gender identity, there was nevertheless a valuable point to be made. Take, for example, the following observations, made when Grabrucker's daughter was 22 months old, and had been on holiday with a boy of similar age and his mother:

> . . . the children have developed one particular set pattern of behaviour. At the start both children are playing happily on their own, then Schorschi stops what he's doing and goes over to Anneli, then there are some variations.
> 1. Schorschi gives Anneli a shove so that she falls over and starts to yell.
> 2. He aims a few blows at her with his hand or some object he's picked up; she starts yelling but he carries on doing this.
> 3. He pushes her over and then hits her; she starts yelling.
> 4. He takes whatever she is playing with away from her; if she holds it tight he takes it away by force. Anneli starts yelling, turns away and comes to me, or else she finds something else to play with. Schorschi now puts the toy he has taken from her down somewhere; it no longer interests him. If Anneli goes on playing, the whole game starts from the beginning again.
> 5. Schorschi goes up to Anneli with some threatening gesture, shouting 'ggrrh' or something similar and pushes Anneli back into the corner of the room. Her shout of 'no' has no effect on him at all.
>
> M. Grabrucker, *There's a Good Girl*, pp. 39–40.

As Grabrucker points out, these sorts of patterns of play between male and female toddlers are extremely common, and are well documented in the research literature. Carol Nagy Jacklin (1983), for example, observed similar scenes in some work with 2-year, 9-month-old children. While she noted many similarities in the play of same-sex pairs, in the case of girl–boy partnerships,

there was very little interaction. We had asked the parents to bring their children to our playroom in play clothes, and although some of these were clearly sex-typed by clothes, we were unable to tell the sex of the children in about half of the cases. Somehow the children seemed to be able to tell, although they never asked each other's names. We have analysed . . . and (tried) to understand the different behaviours in the same and the mixed-sex pairs and have found one interesting difference. If boys use a vocal prohibition such as 'mine' or 'no', their partner is very likely to withdraw or retreat whether their partner is a boy or girl. However, when a girl uses a vocal prohibition, if her partner is a girl she will retreat, but if her partner is a boy, he is not likely to retreat. We do not know what accounts for this difference. . . .

C. N. Jacklin, 'Boys and Girls Entering School', p. 14.

It may be that this is a biologically based difference; perhaps a manifestation of boys' higher level of aggression. If so, so be it. But there is another issue: in order to live in peaceful community with one another, we all of us have to learn to *control* impulses such as aggression. As part of the normal process of growing up, we have to be helped to be sociable, and this applies to aggressive boys as much as to anybody else. Most parents, play leaders and nursery teachers do in fact make efforts to modify obviously anti-social or dangerous behaviour. But there is a level of behaviour just below what would count as clearly unacceptable, which involves snatching toys, monopolising equipment, and so on. And, in my experience as a parent, adults too often allow this sort of thing to go unchallenged. Perhaps because of the prevailing progressive, child-centred approach to the up-bringing of children, adults do not like to appear too authoritarian. As a result, however, some children learn that it is acceptable to do more or less as they like, provided they do not seriously hurt anyone, and others learn that they will have their toys taken and their games spoiled, and adults will leave them to manage as best they can. If you are the parent of a toddler (girl or boy), this is an issue which you are likely to meet, and which you will have to make efforts to resolve. Agree or disagree with Marianne Grabrucker's conclusions – they at least provide some food for thought:

Since adults do not show their disapproval of force or of taking things from others, patterns of behaviour are determined by male children and girls have to fit in with them, whether or not it suits their mood at the time. Girls have to learn to adapt. . . . This seems to me to be a modern variation on an age-old theme. . . . Regardless of how the girl learns to deal with aggressive situations, one thing she does grasp is that she has to learn something, something determined by boys.

M. Grabrucker, *There's a Good Girl*, p. 41

Pre-school education

Although the provision of pre-school education in Britain still lags shamefully behind the rest of Europe, the majority of under-5s do attend some sort of playgroup or nursery before they reach the age of compulsory schooling. The aims and the quality of groups, organisations and individuals catering for this age group vary enormously. What they have in common is that they will all, almost certainly, transmit ideas about male and female behaviour to the children in their care.

More often than not, it is an unconscious and an inevitable process. Like most of the adult population, pre-school teachers use an individual's biological sex, along with other cues, to make basic predictions as to what sort of a person he or she is likely to be. So an adult, operating on the assumption that many little girls are concerned about their appearance, will pass a remark about clothes, or hair, or new shoes in order to break the ice or make a reticent child feel at home. More disturbing from an educational point of view, however, are the *subtle* differences in the ways pre-school staff react to the girls and boys in their charge. Recent observational research by

Julia Hodgeon (*A Woman's World*) in nursery classes in the Cleveland area, for example, indicated that:

1. Girls were offered help more than twice as frequently as boys (62 per cent to 35 per cent).
2. Girls had their intentions probed more often than boys (55 per cent to 33 per cent).
3. Boys were more likely to have their play elaborated (46 per cent to 34 per cent).
4. Boys were more likely to be given information (43 per cent to 30 per cent).
5. Boys were more likely to be directed or managed, with the teacher often checking their behaviour.

It is difficult to know in any absolute sense why the teachers behaved in these ways. But a plausible interpretation, and that favoured by Hodgeon, is that the girls were thought somehow less able to manage, and were viewed more as friends/equals than the boys.

We know, from research carried out in the USA, that pre-school children do come to nursery or playgroup with sex-related preferences for particular play activities, and that little boys are more likely to behave aggressively and disruptively than little girls (L. A. Serbin, 'The Hidden Curriculum'). We know also that unless extreme forms of both boy and girl behaviour are challenged, and gently but firmly channelled into acceptable forms, there may be trouble ahead. From the point of view of little girls, it seems that excessively 'feminine' types score lower on IQ tests than their less conventional peers (E. G. Doherty and C. Culver, 'Sex-role Identification, Ability and Achievement among High School Girls'), and that very compliant, docile and dependent girls may achieve good results at the primary level, but are likely to face problems when education begins to call for a more active, critical and independent orientation.

The picture is complicated by two further issues. First, that compliant, docile and dependent behaviour in girls is seen by many adults as natural, and so is not challenged. And second, that there are playgroups and nurseries founded upon an overly permissive, *laissez-faire* approach where children are allowed to move from one activity to another more or less as they wish. This can mean that there is a sharp division of girls' and boys' activities, and that each sex can go along in its own groove without experiencing the whole range of activities on offer. This is poor preparation for school and for life.

Obviously, some parents do not have access to a playgroup or nursery, and others may have little choice over the one they use. If there is a choice, however, I would always look first and foremost for a caring atmosphere; a vague attribute, perhaps, but easily recognisable when you find it. I once looked over an admirably equipped nursery. With its schedule of activities, and written reports on children's progress, it was designed to appeal to educationally concerned parents. Yet I came away with my two children, feeling distinctly uneasy about the place. I asked my daughter what she thought of it. 'Horrible', she replied. 'Nobody spoke to us.' It was true. Of all the splendidly qualified and uniformed staff, not one had got down to talk to or play with the children. We didn't go back.

Parental preferences as to the issue of structure and discipline will obviously vary, and will also depend upon the personality of the child concerned. From the point of view of preparing children for school, in both social and educational terms, however, there is much to be said for at least a semistructured approach. This allows for the free play and general socialising which all pre-school children need, but also incorporates blocks of organised group activity, where each child is introduced to the range of activities available. This should include at least basic art and craft work, sand and (where possible) water play, access to large toys (ride-on cars, climbing frames, slides, etc.), as well as learning simply to sit still and listen to a story. Some nurseries will also be able to provide a garden, with opportunities to plant and grow, or will take children out for walks. Others will embark on the basics of reading and number work with their older children.

Finally, there is the issue of staffing. While qualifications and training may be taken as a guide, they do not constitute proof that all is satisfactory; personality may provide just as good an indication. Ideally, the two are found in combination. Parents of daughters should not feel afraid to enquire into how the nursery or play group caters for girls. Although such enquiries often produce the stock response that, 'We treat them all the same', or 'We cater for the individual', it is important to go into what this means in practical terms, bearing in mind the issues raised earlier in this chapter. It is worth adding that prospective parents should exercise tact and discretion: nothing is achieved by adopting a neurotic, accusatory manner which puts staff on the defensive. And do look around. Successive governments may have treated pre-school education as the poor relation, but it is widely recognised by educationalists as the cornerstone of learning.

Chapter 3

THE PRIMARY SCHOOL YEARS

First step on the ladder

Most children in Britain begin their formal education, as the law requires, by starting school (or an approved educational programme) around the time of their fifth birthday, some a month or so before, some a little after. As far as the education of girls is concerned the importance of this primary stage has, I believe, been underrated in the past. Because little girls have traditionally achieved good results until at least the age of 11, teachers, parents and educationalists alike have taken the attitude that there is nothing to worry about; that it is the secondary stage that really matters.

Yet for any child, girl or boy, the primary years can be crucial in establishing an orientation to work, and a view of oneself and others. Although these may seem rather abstract concepts, they are part and parcel of the foundations of education: without a positive attitude towards learning, a strong sense of self-worth and developing awareness of the qualities and needs of other people, a child has a shaky start.

So what do we know about girls on this first rung of the educational ladder? How do they perform at primary level, and do schools do well by them? Are there areas in which they may be particularly strong or vulnerable, and how can parents complement the role of the school in providing support and encouragement from home?

Off to school

We know, for a start, that by the time children reach the age of 5, they are generally secure in their sexual identity. In other words, they know that they are either a girl or a boy, and that their biological sex will not change. But their ideas about appropriate behaviour in girls and boys, women and men, are as yet undeveloped. Children of 5, or thereabouts, may well inform you that girls are better at this or that than boys, and vice versa, or that only men/women can do X or Y. But their understanding quite often runs counter to what we, as adults, might expect. If their reasoning is probed, it is found, unsurprisingly, to be based upon their own limited experience, or upon interestingly idiosyncratic logic.

A child of this age is quite capable of claiming, for example, that boys are better at music than girls because 'Philip can play the guitar', or that girls are stronger than boys because 'girls are better at gymnastics'. This does not mean that they have no knowledge of traditional sexual stereotypes. I was told by one 5-year-old girl, whose mother was a doctor, that 'doctors are men'. When I pointed out to her that her own mother was both a woman and a doctor, she thought for a moment before explaining that her mother wasn't a 'proper Mummy'!

So, in short, the child entering school is likely to have *some* notion of sex differences in aptitudes and behaviour, but, typically, to be somewhat confused as to the whys and wherefores.

And the teachers' view?

For their part, teachers are likely to feel that the boys and girls arriving in the reception class behave differently. Depending to some extent upon the catchment area of the school, children will be more or less ready for institutionalised education in terms of their ability to get on with others, sit still, listen to a simple story, take the first steps in reading and writing, and use materials such as pencils, crayons, paper and scissors. And their readiness for these activities may also vary according to sex.

Girls, boys and problems

Although most children of both sexes in fact adapt very quickly to the new demands which school places upon them, boys are more likely than girls both to face and to cause problems. It is important, however, to qualify this statement at once. It is not that all girls are little angels: sensible, co-operative and diligent pupils who never have problems. Or that, by comparison, little boys are disruptive and unruly savages. The general rule (and of course there are always exceptions) is that a small minority of boys experience and create both educational and social difficulties.

The American psychologist Carol Nagy Jacklin has carried out extensive research on sex differences in young children. And she too is at pains to point out that many of the problems we see apply only to a small proportion of the overall population of little boys, suggesting that some of them at least may be due to difficulties and resulting damage caused in labour and childbirth (C. N. Jacklin, 'Boys and Girls Entering School'). Among these problems, she lists hyperactivity (where the ratio of girls to boys categorised as hyperactive varies from 1:5 to 1:20), speech problems, and difficulties with reading.

Certainly, in my own research in infant and junior schools, the pupils who were told off most frequently, or who experienced difficulties with reading and writing (less often with maths) were not boys as a whole, but a small minority; characteristically, three or four boys out of a class of perhaps 20 to 30 pupils. But the forms their problems take can make these boys appear far more than a minority. Running around the classroom, behaving aggressively toward other children, or needing a high level of personal attention from the teacher, for whatever reason, are all essentially disruptive behaviours. They call for a response from the teacher, and they draw her away from other children.

Girls/boys

We also know that it is still common practice in many schools for boys and girls to be divided for such purposes as registration. Feminist critics have long pointed out that this tradition is both antiquated and reactionary. They argue that it would be completely unacceptable to divide children on the basis of race or social class, so why should a sexual division be permitted?

The reason is, simply, that most people find it acceptable. Undoubtedly, institutionalised division on the grounds of race and class is no longer allowed. A teacher would face serious charges if he or she regularly divided the class into blacks and whites, or rich and poor. But to divide people by sex is still almost universally accepted, for reasons which are too complex to unravel here. To my knowledge, there has never been a society which did not, as noted in the previous chapter, observe the difference of biological sex and construct its rules and practices of social gender around it. And the fact that schools, which are a part of society, reflect general attitudes and assumptions in this respect should not surprise us.

What can be disturbing, however, is the way in which some individual teachers *use* this basic form of division. Admittedly, one would be hard pressed to prove the harm in it, in terms of straightforward cause and effect. Yet one questions the educational value of teachers continually setting boys and girls up in competition with one another, using sex-stereotyped characteristics as encouragement, or, especially, using the other sex as a negative reference point: too often when the boy/girl dichotomy enters the fray, we find ourselves express-ing attitudes and resorting to tactics which amplify divisions and work to the detriment of one sex or the other. And in a society where, certainly in terms of money, prestige and power, more value is attached to male characteristics, it is more often than not the girls who are the losers.

We find, for example, boys ridiculed for behaving 'like a load of girls' (a particular favourite on the sports field, this), where femaleness is construed as the negative pole, to be avoided at all costs. Or girls as the victims of the double-edged sword: praised for being conscientious, compliant and docile, which is all very well and undoubtedly makes classroom life easier. But passivity, which is the flip side of conscientiousness, com-pliance and docility, is of no help whatsoever when education begins to call for a critical and inquiring mind.

Now of course, it is easy to over-react to comments which are used casually and with no intention of offence. But, again, I would say that it is just this sort of casual, unintentional behaviour which seeps into the consciousness of those on the receiving end. Good teaching and child-rearing practice, as currently construed, contends that one should lean toward the positive in the education and rearing of children. For this reason, most adults will try to avoid tactics which might undermine a young child's confidence or sense of self-worth. They praise work which, though imperfect, shows evidence of effort, they increase skills by building upon what is good rather than drawing attention to what is bad, and they avoid ridicule and sarcasm. There is no reason why, with a little forethought, these facilities of tact, diplomacy and common sense cannot be brought to bear where issues of sex and gender are involved.

Teacher attention

A large number of observational studies in schools have found that teachers pay more attention to boys than they do to girls (see, for example, J. French and P. French, 'Gender Imbalances in the Primary Classroom'; P. Croll, 'Teacher Interaction with Male and Female Pupils'; V. Morgan and S. Dunn, 'Chameleons in the Classroom'). Again, a general statement like this needs to be qualified, for the term 'attention' is a catch-all category: it can cover anything from spending time discussing a child's work to telling him or her off.

So what can reasonably be said about this issue, and is there real cause for concern? The point should be made once more that in every class where boys get more attention than girls, it is likely to be a few boys, not boys as a whole. And it is also likely that if you were to record the lessons and analyse them in detail (as I have done many times), you would find that the extra attention given to those few boys included a substantial proportion of tellings-off, chivvying to complete work, and general keeping in order.

Keeping the boys in order

On the basis of my own research experience I would suggest that one of the main reasons for teachers giving more attention to boys is, in fact, a disciplinary one. There are two major points to consider.

The first, and it is important to try to see this from the teacher's point of view, is that if a primary school teacher discovers a few potentially troublesome boys in her class she may well find that she has problems on her hands. In some schools, the ratio of teachers to pupils is excellent, and helpers may be provided. But in others, the teacher may find that she is very much on her own; that she has, single-handed, to engage the attention and co-operation of a few difficult pupils as well as to cater for the educational and social needs of the rest of the class. And one way in which teachers do this is to pay more attention to troublesome pupils. They have to do so: if these pupils are ignored or left to their own devices, they can ruin a lesson, and may also annoy, disturb or hurt other children. So, the teacher may find herself paying more attention to troublesome, or potentially troublesome, children than to those who are quiet and conscientious.

The second point is that, on the basis of past experience, reading, college lectures and so on, the teacher may *perceive* boys to pose more of a disciplinary threat. In anticipation of problems, she may then find herself giving more time and attention to boys: hence the tendency observed by some researchers for teachers to choose topics and materials which they know will appeal to boys.

To complicate matters further . . .

It is my belief that we do everybody involved a disservice if we try to over-simplify this issue of teacher attention. In itself it has attracted a lot of attention in both the academic and general press over the years, and has sometimes been over-simplified to the point where one questions the value of discussing it at all. As anybody who has tried seriously to investigate it will attest, it is one of those educational mine-fields which raise more questions than answers, and where our knowledge of both what happens and why it happens is still far from complete.

A case in point . . .

In a research project which we undertook in 1985–86, my husband Peter French and I came up with a number of findings which confirmed observations made in other studies. But we also discovered patterns of behaviour which neither we nor practising teachers could adequately explain, and drew attention to some 'seen-but-unnoticed' aspects of life in classrooms which we found intriguing.

We were funded by the Equal Opportunities Commission to look at patterns of teacher–pupil interaction in the infant school, and had some 278 hours of video-recorded lessons made in a variety of infant schools at our disposal (see J. French and P. French, *Gender Imbalances in Infant School*, for further details). Our specific focus was on discussion time – the time when infant teachers gather the class together to talk about some matter of topical interest. After a preliminary viewing of all the tapes, we isolated 25 clear, good-quality sequences and looked at them in detail. We found that, overall, teachers were more likely to choose boys than girls to take part in the discussion, and also that boys were much more likely than girls to choose themselves (i.e. by calling out) to take part. These patterns are set out in Tables 3.1 and 3.2.

Having made these observations, we turned back to the videotapes to try to find out why they occurred. There was, as we had expected, a great deal of variation from lesson to lesson, but we were able to tease out several tendencies, which operated either on their own, or in conjunction with one another.

One of the most intriguing things we noticed was that, in some of the lessons, boys were quite obviously more *visible* than girls (and see also V. Morgan and S. Dunn, 'Chameleons in the Classroom'). It was standard practice for the teachers to sit themselves on a chair at the front, and to group the children on a carpet or rug at their feet. There were, of course, the usual exceptions but, generally speaking, the girls grouped themselves cross-legged in front of the teacher, and the boys took up places on the margins of the group.

We noticed that the boys were perhaps disposed and certainly able to be more physically restless: they stretched out their legs, or leaned back on their hands, or changed position frequently. Some boys also knelt up, or perched on nearby chairs and tables. By contrast, the girls were still. Overall,

TABLE 3.1 Patterns of pupil participation by sex

Lessons coded alphabetically	A	B	C	D	E	F	G	H	I
Teacher selects girl	7	1	0	8	14	9	12	1	23
Teacher selects boy	18	8	3	9	12	4	9	1	25
Girl self-selects	0	1	0	1	15	0	4	4	0
Boy self-selects	2	1	0	2	12	0	6	12	10

Lessons coded alphabetically	J	K	L	M	N	O	P	Q	R
Teacher selects girl	6	14	6	4	4	5	5	9	5
Teacher selects boy	13	9	13	5	5	7	15	17	12
Girl self-selects	3	3	1	1	1	0	0	0	0
Boy self-selects	12	13	3	6	21	1	0	2	3

Lessons coded alphabetically	S	T	U	V	W	X	Y
Teacher selects girl	2	7	8	6	13	4	11
Teacher selects boy	4	15	6	15	15	6	8
Girl self-selects	1	11	0	0	0	0	0
Boy self-selects	5	12	0	6	2	3	1

this meant that the children most likely to be noticed by the teacher or to catch her eye were boys. The children clustered cross-legged at her feet could be, quite literally, overlooked.

TABLE 3.2 Total numbers of pupil turns by sex

Selection	Girl	Boy
Teacher selects	184	254
Pupil self-selects	46	134
Total no-turns	230	388

It was also clear that some of the boys taking a major part in lessons were lively, eager children whose enthusiasm invited a response. I was reminded of a ball game we used to play at my primary school. We had to form a circle, with the teacher in the middle. She used to toss the ball to one or another of the pupils, who threw it back. It was then thrown to another child, and so on. The idea was, I suppose, to speed up our reactions as well as improving our throwing and catching skills. The thing about this game was that as soon as the ball came towards you, teacher or pupil, you had to react. And that was what struck me most forcibly about the teachers I watched on the videotapes: they had to respond to the input they were getting from the children. It is a mistake to think of lessons as some sort of one-way sermon with the teacher in sole charge. Children also participate. This is why the same lesson, given to different groups of children, can be such a different experience for the teacher.

That question of order – again

Like other researchers before us, we too found that, even at the infant level, boys were involved in issues of discipline more often than girls. We examined a subset of occasions where teachers dealt with such problems as speaking out of turn, lapses in attention and children either fidgeting in or leaving their seats. We found 104 occasions where these disciplinary issues arose, and in 97 cases it was possible to tell whether a girl or boy was involved. As Tables 3.3, 3.4, 3.5 and 3.6 show, boys had to be admonished or otherwise dealt with far more frequently than girls.

TABLE 3.3 Distribution between girls and boys of all disciplinary talk

	Boy addressee	Girl addressee	Indeterminate	Total
No. of instances	74	23	7	104
% of total	71.85	22.12	6.73	100

(Binomial score $z = 7.4628$; $p < 0.001$)

TABLES 3.4, 3.5, 3.6 Behavioural problems addressed by pupil sex

3.4	Inattention	3.5	Seating Posture	3.6	Turn-taking
Boys	29	Boys	31	Boys	15
Girls	9	Girls	9	Girls	2
Total	38	*Total*	40	*Total*	17
($z = 0.0003$; $p < 0.0001$)		($z = 0.0014$; $p < 0.01$)		($z = 0.0001$; $p < 0.001$)	

An additional and curious finding which came out of this particular line of inquiry was that the teachers tended to *structure* their reprimands differently, according to the sex of the child involved. If a little girl was, say, kneeling or standing when she should have been sitting, or talking when she should have been listening, teachers would use formulations such as:

> 'Sit down Lisa, love' or
> 'Could you stop talking now, dear?'

A little boy doing the same thing would get:

> 'You sit down *and then we can all see*', or
> 'Can you stop talking now dear, *so that I can hear what the other children are saying.*'

Sometimes, too, teachers would fall short of actually telling children how to behave. Instead they simply stated that a child's current behaviour was problematic, and the child was left to work out what was wrong and amend it accordingly. And where this happened, boys were again more likely to have an explanation tagged on. Girls, on the other hand, were more likely to have some sort of negative description of their behaviour added (e.g. 'you're being silly').

We puzzled over these patterns which, frankly, surprised us, and spoke to a number of experienced teachers about them. None of us had been aware of this particular sex difference before, and although we came up with several plausible explanations, none was definitive:

1. Do teachers prefer boys?

Some feminist studies have suggested that teachers prefer boys, and that they are less tolerant of bad behaviour when girls as opposed to boys are involved. Was the patterning which we had uncovered an instance of this alleged preference in action?

2. Same-sex identification?

Was it perhaps that the teachers (all of whom in this particular sub-investigation were female) assumed that the girls, as females like themselves, knew the rules and the reasons behind them?

3. Docile rule-followers?

Do teachers perhaps see girls as more compliant? If so, they might assume that they can safely dispense with explanations – the girls will comply anyway. Boys, however, might question the teacher's authority and, therefore, in the cause of expediency, explanations are attached.

4. A question of maturity?

Are girls seen as more socially adept and mature, so that rules do not have to be explained more than once? And are boys, by the same token, seen as needing repetitive restatement?

I do not know the answer, but the very fact that the question has to be asked shows the subtlety which may sometimes characterise our differential treatment of the sexes. This does not mean that we are always so subtle or mysterious. Other classroom-based studies have pointed to more obvious ways in which teachers treat girls and boys differently.

Lesson topics

Since the late 1960s, most state-maintained primary schools have worked with an integrated, multi-disciplinary approach to knowledge. In other words, they have not had a strict time-table, with slots for geography, history, English, and so on. Instead, teachers have developed schemes of work based around topics thought relevant to the children's abilities, needs and interests at a particular time. Different perspectives, representing the various subject disciplines, are then brought to bear on the topic chosen. A scheme of work on the Vikings, for instance, would include historical and geographical information, art work, examples of literature, and so on; all so as to give a broad, general picture of Nordic civilisation, its major features and achievements and its impact upon the indigenous British population.

Critics of this multi-disciplinary approach have always argued, on general educational grounds, that it is too much of a hit-and-miss affair. Until the 1988 Education Reform Act, and the advent of the National Curriculum, choice of topics rested largely with the teacher. This meant that children could cover a single topic several times in different classes, could miss some areas altogether, and could therefore end up with a very patchy grasp of, say, historical development.

Doubts have also been expressed on sex-related grounds. In 'Dinosaurs in the Classroom', a paper published in 1978 which had a great impact in educational circles at the time and is still widely quoted, Kathy Clarricoates pointed out that teachers were more likely to choose topics which they knew would capture the attention and interest of the boys. Hence the popularity of themes such as Dinosaurs, or, for that matter, Vikings!

With the benefit of hindsight, it seems a commonplace observation. Yet I remember that, when I read it, it set me thinking about my own practice as a student and as a young teacher. My memories made me squirm! I particularly remember my tutor on first-year teaching practice suggesting I cover the theme Transport. 'You could get them to make a frieze', he explained. 'A street scene. The boys could do the cars, planes, motorbikes, transporters . . . ' (he was enjoying the prospect himself by this time). 'And the girls can do the houses.'

On a second-year teaching practice, I joined a class on an outing to the fire station where the girls, quite literally, took a back seat in the fire engines. On the way back to school one of them complained that their teacher would never think of taking them to visit a hospital so that they could see some of the work done by nurses. This, she thought, was because the boys would not be interested. Yet they, the girls, were expected to 'tag along' to the fire station.

Now, of course, one could argue, as I did, that seeing how fire stations operate is of some general interest. But she had a point. It would not have occurred to her teacher to get a nurse or a hairdresser or a secretary to talk to them. To a sub-group of girls, perhaps. But boys would not have been expected to listen.

I saw, and still see, this little cameo repeated in schools. Because they have a few potentially troublesome boys, teachers, perhaps quite unconsciously, plan lessons so as to capture and keep their interest, select topics which they know have boy-appeal, and use anecdotes and examples to the same ends.

Literature

Again during the 1970s, observers began to point out that females were grossly under-represented in many of the books found in primary school classrooms. As noted in the previous chapter, Glenys Lobban made a close study of some of the most popular reading schemes of the time. She reported that not only were females thin on the ground in these schemes, they were also represented in a very restricted number of roles. Princesses and witches abounded in the realms of fantasy, while real-life characters were either mothers, teachers, or nurses! The Ladybird series in particular was castigated for its outlook, which was not only sexist, but, to add insult to injury, racist and classist as well.

Over the past twenty years, this situation has improved dramatically. Some of the children's reading schemes now available carry realistic story-lines, use credible characters of both sexes, everyday as well as fantasy settings, and are also beautifully illustrated. Yet, as noted earlier, there is often a time-lag in the availability of books and their purchase by schools. Sometimes, too, a scheme will be retained simply because it works.

The issue of under-representation of females also applies in relation to fictional literature which may be read to the children or, as they become more proficient readers, by the children themselves. It may be seen, too, in works of non-fiction, particularly in the case of the natural sciences, where, in older books at any rate, girls are too often depicted in a passive or background role, if at all.

As with younger children, there is a case for parents introducing books in which girls do feature as more than supportive props for the boys. And certainly parents should feel able to discuss, with both boys and girls, the ways in which male and female characters are depicted and story-lines developed in the books that they read.

Looking to the future: the National Curriculum

The National Curriculum is one of the major changes to our education system implemented under the 1988 Education Reform Act. It is being phased in gradually and will mean, eventually, that all children between the ages of 5 and 16 in maintained (state) schools will study the three *core* subjects of English, maths, and science, together with the seven *foundation* subjects of history, geography, a foreign language, music, art, physical education, and technology. The passage of the National Curriculum from initial proposal to legislation has been by no means plain sailing. The programmes of study in some of the subjects have yet to be finalised, the history syllabus caused major controversy, and debate continues as to how older pupils are going to manage their GCSE *and* their National Curriculum subjects.

But from the point of view of girls, the overall outlook has to be seen as positive. Under the old option system, most secondary school children were allowed to drop particular subjects at the end of the second or third year. As we shall see in the next chapter, this meant that many girls dropped the sciences and technology, and so cut themselves off from a whole range of future occupational areas. It also meant that their education was incomplete: girls who had little or no knowledge of the sciences and modern technology were ill-equipped for life in late-twentieth-century society. Under the National Curriculum, girls as well as boys will have to study the whole range of subjects, and this will begin at the *primary level*.

I see this latter fact as very important. All too often, it is boys who are perceived to display an interest in matters scientific and technological. Their interest is developed and their confidence and expertise increased through both home experience (the provision of particular toys and equipment, for example) and school experience (if boys are permitted to monopolise the computers or scientific/technological apparatus, for example). As we have seen in the book so far, if girls do not display similar interest, few people are unduly concerned. Under the National Curriculum, the interest which I believe all children, regardless of sex, have in the natural world, how things work, and why certain phenomena occur will have to be harnessed in girls as well as boys. For many girls, this is going to open doors to a range of experiences and spheres of knowledge which, in the past, effectively bore signs reading 'Restricted Entry'.

The fact that this is set to happen in schools is also likely to have a knock-on effect in homes. For not only are girls likely to express more interest in matters which have usually, although perhaps unconsciously, been labelled the domain of boys, but *parents themselves* are going to come under pressure to support their daughters in school-based projects and investigations. This is likely to change parental perceptions, and to begin to provide daughters as well as sons with the encouragement, the practice, the out-of-school visits and experiences, and the overall support which lay the necessary foundations for future competence. For these reasons, I look forward to seeing an increase in the numbers of girls following scientific and technological careers and, just as importantly, to girls knowing something of and feeling comfortable in the worlds of science and technology in the years to come.

Parents and schools

The 1988 Education Act also gives parents the potential for greater than ever involvement in their children's schools. Under the system of Local Management, phased in from 1 April 1990, governing bodies rather than local education authorities become responsible for the financial and organisational management of schools, and for ensuring that the requirements of the National Curriculum are fulfilled. Competition between schools also looks set to become more intense, as test and examination results are made public, and children who have the means to travel are not effectively obliged to attend their local schools. Many educationalists have their reservations about these policies: judging schools by their academic results alone, for example, may lead to schools in already disadvantaged areas losing their most enthusiastic and educable pupils. But thinking again of the special case of girls, the greater involvement of parents, and the increased pressure on schools to consider the parental point of view, may ensure that the particular issues affecting girls are made known to and considered by the governing body. The ball is well and truly in the parents' court.

Chapter 4
MOVING ON

The transfer to secondary education

The vast majority of British school children transfer from the primary to the secondary phase of education at the age of 11. It can be a difficult period. Most children move from a relatively small, intimate environment to a much larger, less personal one. From being the oldest and biggest children in the school, they are suddenly transformed into the youngest and smallest. And some of them are also in the throes of puberty. Little wonder that it is often a time of stress for both children and their parents.

The top junior class

Top junior classes have a number of characteristics in common. Apart from awareness of their status as the top class, children of this age often develop more equal relationships with teachers, take on positions of responsibility within the school, and so on. It is also probable that their class, as a unit, has been together for some time. The children all know one another well, there are strong friendships, personal strengths and weaknesses are acknowledged. And, although it is by no means common to all children, there is an air of confidence and expectation as the end of the summer term approaches.

The 'characters'

My own observations in top junior classes have often included the fact that there are usually a number of what have been described to me by teachers as 'characters' (see J. French and P. French, 'Gender Imbalances in the Primary Classroom'). Known to everyone, these children frequently have a talent to amuse: they are witty and spontaneous, engage in entertaining banter and repartee with the teacher, they clown around, and are at the centre of whatever type of plot or subterfuge is currently doing the rounds. Occasionally, they are female. Usually, they are male.

Undoubtedly, the presence of one or more characters in a class influences the dynamics of the group – the ways in which children relate to one another and the teacher, and the way in which the teacher relates to the class – to no small extent. Without, and even with, a strong-willed teacher, they can set the tone of lessons, and, by sheer force of personality, relegate other children to the shade. This means that both less ebullient boys and the majority of the girls are transformed into a sort of audience, or backcloth to the activities of a small minority.

Some teachers, educationalists, and parents would argue that this is simply a fact of life: that it is inevitable for certain children to assume dominant and others subordinate positions. They are probably right, to a certain extent. But the *degree* to which it is allowed to happen within an educational context is the crucial matter for debate. As children reach the top end of the junior school, make the transfer to secondary education and begin the long haul towards GCSE, it becomes a question of both social and educational importance, and it is a theme which I develop and return to in this and the following chapter.

The onset of puberty

As the end of primary education approaches, physical differences as well as those of character and outlook also become more obvious. Some girls may be beginning to develop breasts and may have started their periods. Because of the ambivalence of the surrounding culture to these changes, this can be a source of embarrassment or, at the least, increased self-consciousness for them. Activities such as changing for PE or swimming can take on a new significance, while coping with periods within the school context can be a nightmare.

For many girls, this time of transition sadly marks the end of carefree childhood and, if it is handled badly, can adversely affect all areas of life. It is important, therefore, for parents to inform the school if a daughter has begun her periods, or started to wear a bra: she may have to use staff toilets, and may feel the need for greater privacy to get changed. Staff cannot make such provisions, or even be aware of the need for greater tact and discretion if they do not know of the circumstances.

Perhaps the greatest change which comes over girls at this stage is a general sense of vulnerability, and awareness of their emerging sexuality. Some have every appearance of thriving on it, but for others, perhaps most, it is a time of trial and ambivalent feelings. It is also a time when sexual harassment can become a problem.

The peer group

Peer group pressure for both boys and girls at this age is approaching its height. In fact, this is often the time when parents find that the close relationships they have had with their children become strained, as the children become young people, not with minds of their own but with what appears to be a collective consciousness! But although parents may feel excluded, close friendships, which are often same-sex, can positively help adolescents through the troubled waters of the early teenage years.

Problems arise, however, if the peer group is thought by parents to be a bad influence: if there is evidence of a particular group of youngsters engaging in anti-social behaviour, experimenting with drink or drugs, and where education seems to be the least of their concerns.

For girls, there is the additional issue of body-image, a concern aided and abetted by the teen magazine industry which all too often appears to think about little else. For a combination of psychological, social and cultural reasons, girls (and, apparently, increasing numbers of boys) can become obsessed with the idea that they are overweight. Some go on to develop disorders such as anorexia nervosa, in which they slim compulsively and often surreptitiously until their appearance is excessively wasted, and specialist help is required. Others develop habits of bingeing and then making themselves vomit (bulimia). While these disorders represent the extreme end of the spectrum, there is no doubt that issues of weight, and of appearance more generally, can become preoccupations of adolescent girls, and that the flames can be fanned within a like-minded peer group.

The question of relationships with boys and men is also likely to loom large from this stage onwards. There is great variation in the way girls and boys handle this aspect of growing up, depending on personality and surrounding circumstances. Sometimes, relationships evolve quite naturally from friendships based on mutually held attitudes or interests, and any parent who notices this happening can surely sigh with relief. More often, there is anxiety and upset as adolescents put themselves through painful courtship rituals, whereby it is made known (usually by a third party!) that X 'fancies' Y, Y humiliates X because he or she fancies Z, and so on! Or there is the situation where girls refuse to have anything whatsoever to do with boys of their own age on the grounds that they are 'immature', and transfer their affections to older boys, actors and entertainers, or, sometimes, teachers. These objects of affection usually have in common the fact that they are unattainable, and can inspire a slavish devotion which is alarming for parents to behold. Usually, it passes, but it can take some time, and, again, can be helped or hindered by the peer group.

The central problem for girls at this stage in their development as people is, I think, that they can become entirely absorbed in the business of being female, a process which is without parallel in the case of boys. There are, for example, scores of girls' magazines which concentrate upon appearance, boyfriends and the world of entertainment, reflecting, no doubt, a persistent demand for them. There are no equivalent magazines, jam-packed with hints on how to 'look good, feel good' or 'lose those extra inches' or 'catch and keep' a girlfriend, for the boys! It is expected and it is generally the case, that adolescent boys will develop an interest in females, and will want, at some level, to be attractive to them, but it is also assumed that they will continue to be interested in matters other than simply being a boy.

The individual response to adolescence

Individuals respond differently to adolescence, although their response is affected not only by personality, but also by other, usually related factors, such as social class, ethnic or religious grouping, neighbourhood and environment, and peer group. Obviously this response will in turn affect the way a child responds to school. It is very difficult to predict, as they move on from primary to secondary education, what children will be like in two, three, or four years' time and, accordingly, which school would be best for them. Of course, for many parents the question of choosing a secondary school does not arise: their children automatically go to the local school. But under the 1988 Education Reform Act's policy of open enrolment, parents will have a wider choice available, and children will no longer effectively have no alternative but to go to the school in whose catchment area they live.

Attempts under the same Act to involve parents more closely in the running and management of schools may mean that more parents become involved and interested in their children's education. Alternatively, it may mean that the sorts of parents who are already interested may become more closely involved. In either case, and with open enrolment, it is likely that more parents will actively participate in choosing rather than being allocated a school.

In the case of a girl, this process should involve consideration of the particular pitfalls of female adolescence, as well as the usual assessment of a school according to its academic suitability and overall philosophy and ethos. And it is to a discussion of these combined factors that we now turn.

Chapter 5

THE SECONDARY STAGE

So, as children move towards the top end of the primary school, the time comes for parents to think about what is going to happen next. Whether you are in the position of choosing a school for your daughter, trying to influence policy in relation to your local school, or trying, simply, to be a supportive parent, the following points are worth considering.

Your daughter

Parents should never forget that they know their own children better than anybody else. Granted, we do not see them in the classroom or the playground in interaction with large numbers of other children of the same age. But we have been intimately involved in their growth and development, watched as they make and break friends, seen how they respond to new challenges, cope with other children, and out-of-school activities, noticed what they enjoy and what they find difficult. . . . The list is endless. Most of the time, we take our perceptions for granted; we think of them, perhaps, as the natural observations of any caring parent rather than as 'professional' knowledge. But this does not mean that our perceptions have no value: on the contrary. A good and/or experienced teacher will always take account of what a parent has to say and will work in partnership to bring out the best in an individual child.

This means that when it comes to thinking about secondary education, your impressions as a parent are important. What is your daughter like? Is she an extrovert? Or is she the sort of child who keeps herself to herself? Is she old or young for her years, and in what sense? Does she seem to cope well with other children, or is she cowed by them? What are her friends like, and how important are they to her (or you)? Has she been the victim of bullying or malice, or has she, to your knowledge, ever bullied or been seriously unkind to another child? How is she in academic terms? You may think that she is exceptionally bright, but do her teachers? How has she compared with other children? Are there subject areas in which she excels or is struggling? Does she have a particular talent; in music, sport, art, drama or, perhaps, in a hobby or activity which she has pursued outside school? If so, is this talent likely to develop further? Is she so good as to need a specialist school? How would her local secondary school be able to cater for her? In other words, and be honest, what sort of a person is she?

The above list of questions is by no means exhaustive, but it does provide some pointers as to the sorts of issues to consider. The next step is to think about your daughter in relation to:

The local secondary school

Having built up a picture of your daughter, the next thing is to do the same in relation to your local school. You probably have some idea as to its standing in the community simply from being around it and talking to other parents, but it is worth making the effort to find out for yourself and form your own impressions. If there is an open day, go along. Talk to the staff, talk to the pupils, look around the school, look at the children's work, read the school brochure or prospectus.

Is it a large or small school?

Many secondary schools nowadays are very large, and can appear daunting to a shy 11-year-old. They need not, however, be the anonymous institutions which many parents fear them to be. Much will depend on how the school is organised, and the personalities of staff. Is there an upper and lower school, with a head for each? How are the forms organised, and will your child have a chance to get to know her form teacher? Are there form periods when children can discuss school matters with the form teacher, or is the form teacher/pupil relationship limited to the taking of the register? Are there small tutor groups where children can talk over anything which is worrying them, or is there a friendly member of staff to whom they can turn? In other words, how is the pastoral side of the children's education regarded and organised?

What is its academic standing?

Because of the way our towns and cities are laid out, and schools situated within communities, it is quite possible to find two schools within a short distance of one another with noticeably different records of academic achievement. This happens because of the relationship of social class to educational attainment. Put very simply, the children of unskilled manual workers have far less chance of doing well at school and going on to university than the children of highly qualified professional people. We cannot discount the possibility that inherited ability plays some part in what is a very complex equation, but issues of confidence, feeling at home in the educational environment, orientation to work, and enjoying the right sort of support from home all play their part. So, when a school is situated within a comparatively poor neighbourhood, and draws its pupils primarily from that area, it is likely to produce less glowing academic results than a school in a prosperous area which draws almost all its pupils from its immediate surroundings.

This is to simplify what is, however, an extremely complicated issue, and parents who find themselves having to give thought to it are well advised to consider the case of their local school/s on their own merits. We know, for example, that leadership from the headteacher and commitment from teaching staff can make a tremendous difference, so that a school in a 'poor' neighbourhood can actually do very well by its pupils. By the same token, a school in a 'good' neighbourhood may once have produced very good results and built up a reputation accordingly. Is it still doing so well, or is it resting on its laurels, so to speak?

Under the 1988 Education Reform Act, all children in state schools are required to take tests at the ages of 7, 11, 14 and 16. Although some of the details relating to these tests are still being finalised, it looks very much as though the results of each school will be made public. And, of course, the results of GCSE and A-level examinations are also available to parents. Both test and examination results will provide some indication of the school's achievements, but the importance of taking into account factors such as catchment area, parental attitudes and the ethos of the school will still be of great significance.

The headteacher

As suggested in the previous section, the headteacher bears an enormous responsibility for all that goes on in a school. Obviously, he or she cannot be held personally accountable for the behaviour of individual children: as they grow older, children have to accept responsibility for their own actions. But the head's influence should be felt. It is worth listening to the headteacher's address if there is an open day, reading his/her message in the school magazine, listening to what staff and pupils have to say. And if there is an opportunity to have a chat, take it.

The ethos of the school

Inevitably, gaining an impression of a headteacher is something of a hit or miss affair, and no guarantees can be given. But headteachers undoubtedly make a difference to a school, most notably in terms of its ethos and underlying approach to learning. Some schools, for example, are more overtly committed to competition than others. Some emphasise the non-academic side of education as well as the need to see results. Others, whatever their overall ethos or philosophy, have a strong sense of community as a school, and will quickly make a newcomer feel at home. Yet others have developed strong ties with the local community, or with industry, and will provide an open and all-embracing rather than an 'enclosed' education, which will appeal to many parents.

Obviously, your child will be better suited to the atmosphere and the philosophy of some schools than others. This is why it is important not to dismiss school brochures, but to read them and to assess the mood of the institution where your child may, after all, spend a considerable portion of the next five years or so of her life.

It is also worth making the very obvious point that what suits you may not suit your child. There are parents who, come hell or high water, want their children to go to a particular type of school, a tendency seen particularly in respect of the independent sector, where family traditions are at stake. So decidedly unsporty children find themselves in alarmingly sporty schools, non-academic children are forced into hot-house establishments which leave them feeling inadequate and unhappy, and musical children find themselves in the company of philistines who think that anyone who has even heard of Mozart deserves to be disembowelled behind the bicycle shed!

The message must be to think of the child, first and foremost. If there is any doubt, or if the child shows no particular strengths or weaknesses, look for a good, liberal school which allows its pupils to experience the full range of subjects within a balanced atmosphere of competition, co-operation and respect for others.

The other pupils

The headteacher plays his or her part in determining the ethos of a school; so too do the pupils. It is helpful to meet pupils and to talk to them about their impressions of the school. Open days often provide an excellent opportunity for this. It is also worth noting the behaviour of pupils outside the school. What is the policy at lunch time, for example? Would you prefer your child to eat in the school dining room and remain on the school premises, or do you think she should have the freedom to buy and eat food outside the school? How do the children behave in the community, on the buses, on the streets? It is important to get a fair impression. Do not, for example, write off a whole school because of the behaviour of one or two pupils: try to look at the majority.

There is also the issue of the school's catchment area, and the socio-economic and racial backgrounds of pupils. There are some parents who feel strongly that they want their children to go to schools with as rich a mix of pupils as possible. This, they feel, enables their children to get along with anybody, and to make friends across religious or social barriers.

Others feel equally strongly that they do not want their children to be held back by pupils who cannot speak English, or who are simply not interested in academic achievement. Too often, concerns such as these are summarily dismissed by educationalists. Certainly, if parents are motivated by racism or class prejudice, pure and simple, there is little point in trying to tease out their worries or reason with them. But the fear that one's children may be disadvantaged in academic terms by their fellow pupils does need to be taken seriously. On this point, it is worth bearing in mind that by the time they reach secondary age, those pupils who do not speak English as their mother tongue will be proficient speakers of two or more languages. And that the presence of racial minorities in a school does not necessarily pull standards down: on the contrary, it may improve them. A recent London-based study showed, for example, that children of Indian parentage achieved better examination results than other racial groups, including the white British.

There is, of course, no simple answer to this question. The message must be that when choosing a secondary school, parents have to identify and assess all the important factors. Given the importance of the peer group to children of this age, it is hypocritical to pretend that one's fellow pupils do not matter and should play no part in the reckonings. They do and they should. Again, parents should take heart from the fact that they know their own children, and the paramount aim must be to provide the conditions in which those children will thrive.

The special case of girls

The issues covered so far could apply as well to boys as to girls. But there are several important points which particularly affect girls at this stage in their educational careers, and which should be considered as they make the transition from primary to secondary education.

Staffing at the secondary stage

It is noticeable that male staff occupy more positions of responsibility in secondary schools than do females. Most headteachers are male, most heads of department are male, and where females are found in positions of leadership, it is often within traditionally female spheres of influence, such as the lower school, the arts, humanities or domestic subjects (see S. Acker, 'Women and Teaching'; R. G. Burgess, 'Something You Learn to Live with?'). There is, of course, the question of how we value these spheres of influence. And without a doubt, areas which have traditionally been more the domain of women than men have been grossly undervalued in the past. There is, therefore, a need to rethink and upgrade our attitudes to these areas. At the same time, girls do need to see, as part of their everyday experience, women in positions of responsibility and authority in relation to both traditional and non-traditional subjects.

This is one point on which girls' schools win hands down. Most girls' schools are led by a head*mistress*, and the majority of staff, including heads of department, chemistry, physics and technology teachers, are female. Girls thus automatically absorb the idea that women can and do lead, and not just within the traditionally female subject areas. This perhaps goes some way to explaining the observation made by R. R. Dale, in his three-volume study, *Mixed or Single-sex School?*, in the late 1960s and early 1970s, that girls who had attended girls' schools were less willing than their counterparts from the co-educational sector to work under the authority of a male boss!

It is, therefore, worth looking at the staffing situation in a prospective school, and inquiring specifically as to female representation. Even if the current situation is male dominated, a (tactfully framed) inquiry such as this can put the staffing issue on the agenda, and can pave the way for a more balanced ratio in the future.

The question of male–female balance on the staff is closely related to that of teacher attitudes. A disturbing study by Michelle Stanworth, *Gender and Schooling*, based in a mixed-sex college of further education, disclosed several worrying trends. Using a combination of interviews with staff and students, and observation of A-level lessons, she noted that girls may be directed toward less demanding careers than their abilities merit. One very able girl, ranked as the top performer in both her main subjects, and who had her sights set on a career in the diplomatic service, was envisaged by a male teacher as 'personal assistant to somebody rather important'. By contrast, Stanworth points out that 'boys – even those in danger of failing their examinations – were seen in jobs involving considerable responsibility and authority'. One boy, whose essays had been described as 'bald, childlike and undeveloped', was viewed as rising to head-office status.

At the same time, staff admitted that they did not know their female pupils very well, in part because they were overshadowed in class by more extrovert and vociferous boys. One teacher rather disparagingly referred to the girls in his class as a 'faceless bunch', and his less than confidence-enhancing attitudes were reflected in the attitudes of the students themselves. The boys spoke disdainfully of the girls' reticence, cast aspersions on their academic ability (even where records of achievement indicated that it was better than the boys' own) and character, and the girls' responses likewise indicated a profound lack of confidence and self-respect.

Now, of course, it is difficult to generalise from these observations. They are sufficiently disturbing, however, to warrant serious consideration on the part of both teachers and parents. Parents choosing a school for a daughter might quite legitimately inquire as to whether there is a policy of providing equal opportunity. If so, how is it realised in terms of teachers' attitudes? If there is not – and some schools are suspicious of grand-sounding labels which can turn out to mean very little – parents are still entitled to express their concerns and for them to be addressed. The outcome of such inquiries will naturally depend on the way in which they are framed. Aggressive, accusatory tactics are likely to receive short shrift. Diplomatic and constructive queries should achieve results.

Sexual harassment

In 1985, a book by Pat Mahony, *Schools for the Boys?*, on the issue of co-education and its effect on girls was the subject of considerable media coverage. One of the chapters deals in some detail with the subject of sexual harassment of girls by boys in mixed schools, and it was this aspect of the book which, of course, was seized upon as good, newsworthy copy. Mahony contends that girls are habitually subject to outright verbal abuse and vilification, to physical molestation and to more subtle forms of behaviour which, although less overtly hostile, nevertheless carry the same message: that girls are less important and less socially valuable than boys.

Whether one agrees wholeheartedly, or feels that she overstates her case, there is here an issue worthy of consideration. To my mind, the most disturbing aspect of it is the acceptance by staff as normal what amount to appalling standards of behaviour within a school community, and the sense that the girls must adapt their lives so as to avoid situations where harassment of one sort or another is likely to occur. For some girls in the school Mahony observed, this meant leaving lessons early so as to clear the area before the boys were released, or remaining secluded in their own common room until lessons were just about to begin, so as to avoid verbal and physical abuse in the crush on corridors and staircases. There is of course a sense in which the sexual harassment of females by males is a fact of life within our society, and everybody has to learn to deal with it. But where it enters into the world of education, opinion on how to tackle it may differ.

Some parents will take the view that girls have to learn to cope. They will advise their daughters to 'ignore it', or 'give as good as you get', or 'sort it out', according to their own upbringing and attitudes. Others will feel that although some degree of banter is inevitable, sexual hostility and abuse are unacceptable. Unfortunately, the only way of establishing whether or not this is a serious problem within a school is to try it and see. If it then transpires that it is, parents must make this known, and the matter must be investigated. Some schools have a policy of challenging hostile behaviour to subgroups of pupils through the medium of social studies programmes specifically designed for that purpose. While most parents would agree with the ideals of tolerance and liberalism which such policies seek to promote, some feel that these ideals should inform and permeate the curriculum rather than having their own particular and, as some see it, time-wasting slot.

Whatever one's view, it is worth considering the question of sexual harassment, and trying to gauge its incidence and seriousness within a school. While there is always likely to be a level of sexual consciousness and awareness among children of this age, girls should not have to pursue their education in an atmosphere of hostility and disrespect. A parent whose daughter is experiencing this sort of problem should have no reservations about approaching the school and asking for the matter to be investigated; or, where appropriate, about insisting that the boy or boys responsible are challenged and admonished, and *their* behaviour, rather than the girls', is modified.

Interaction in classrooms

Research conducted in secondary school classrooms has suggested that, as in primary classrooms, boys tend to have the lion's share of teachers' attention, and to receive rather different forms of attention from girls (again, for example, they are reprimanded more frequently than girls). Although both the research findings and, it has to be said, the quality of the studies themselves do vary, it has been generally accepted in recent years that in the secondary classroom boys have about two-thirds of the speaking turns, and girls a third. These figures have recently been disputed by some Australian researchers (B. C. Dart and J. A. Clarke, 'Sexism in Schools'), who, after looking at the literature, argued that the studies were so different in scope and methodology that no such general statement could possibly be seen as reliable. While there is a need for further, careful research, there are also, I believe, grounds for concern among those who have the interests of girls at heart.

I have not, personally, conducted a great deal of observational research at the secondary level, but what I have seen has convinced me both that there is a case to answer, and that further study of particular issues is necessary. As part of a wider investigation of girls and science and technology (the Manchester-based Girls into Science and Technology project – see A. Kelly, *Final Report*; J. Whyte, *Girls into Science and Technology* for further details), I went into a school in the Greater Manchester area and video-recorded a series of first-year science lessons. In all, the videos amounted to three hours' material; not enough to form a general picture, but enough to highlight some matters of interest and concern which warrant further investigation.

I observed a mixed-sex, first-year group of 23 pupils (12 girls, 11 boys) involved in a series of experiments linked by the theme 'Heating'. The teacher was a woman, fully aware of my interests, and herself committed to girls following the sciences. The school was in a pleasant, prosperous area, with a majority of supportive parents and interested pupils. In the lessons I observed there were no serious disciplinary problems, and no sense of an anti-school atmosphere. The teaching was of a high quality and the teacher appeared to enjoy a good relationship with the children.

Yet still, in this situation where all the surrounding factors pointed to girls achieving good results, all was not well. I noticed as I recorded the lessons, and had my impressions confirmed by subsequent analysis of the videotapes, that half a dozen dominant boys were answering most of the questions, drawing the diagrams on the blackboard and performing the demonstration experiments. They were by no stretch of the imagination difficult boys. On the contrary, two at least appeared to be very bright and all were obviously keen, interested, and eager to be involved. In personality terms, they seemed pleasant and courteous, occasionally teasing one another and their classmates, but I saw no evidence of malice or sexually explicit harassment in the lessons I observed. As a former teacher myself, I could quite see why the teacher enjoyed teaching them.

The girls and the remaining boys formed a distinct contrast.

Although they observed the experiments conscientiously, noted down the work quietly, and performed the tasks required of them, they had none of the sparky spontaneity and enthusiasm of the dominant boys. None of the girls volunteered to draw a diagram on the blackboard or to perform the experiment for the class, a fact of which the teacher became suddenly aware about twenty minutes into the lesson. She then suggested that when the three boys had performed the demonstration experiment, 'We'll get one or two of the girls, who don't usually volunteer to do the experiments, to comment on our demonstration, shall we?' Now, of course, much could be made of the teacher's use of the terms 'we' and 'our' in this context, the suggestion being that the teacher implicitly groups herself and the boys together as 'us' with 'our scientific concerns' while the girls are excluded as 'other'. But it is also interesting to note that the girls, by the teacher's own admission, did not usually volunteer to do the experiments. And this fitted in with my subsequent observations of them as passive spectators of what was going on around them.

At a later stage in the same lesson, the teacher asked pupils to name the apparatus needed for the experiment, which they were now about to try for themselves in small groups, and to dictate to her the method, which she then wrote on the blackboard for them to copy. At this point, I noticed, and again my impressions were confirmed by analysis, that the girls were volunteering to answer and, indeed, were answering the teacher's questions. But it struck me that the *type* of question they were answering was the least intellectually demanding of the questions posed in the course of the lesson. They were involved, for example, in naming and listing the equipment needed for the experiment, which was laid out on the teacher's bench in front of them and simply needed to be itemised, and in recounting the steps in the method, which they had already seen performed and which had also been rehearsed by the teacher. The questions which involved inference from one experiment to another, prediction, or generalisation were, in this lesson and the others, all answered by boys.

Obviously, my limited observation of this area cannot be

taken as representing a general picture. But at the same time, the fact that these tendencies were in evidence is disquieting. In science, as in all subjects where practical and theoretical knowledge go hand in hand, and where expertise and understanding are built up lesson by lesson, success depends to some extent upon an active approach to learning. And this orientation, where children have the confidence to sound out their ideas, and to make mistakes, becomes more and more important as they work toward GCSE or A level. Certainly, in the lessons I saw, none of the girls had this orientation. This was not, I am sure, because they were of deficient intellect: rather, it is connected with the dynamics of mixed-sex interaction at this adolescent stage of life. Increasingly, teachers are aware of this as an issue, and some schools have experimented with single-sex groups in science and mathematics (see, for example, A. Kelly, *The Missing Half*; S. Smith, *Separate Tables?* and *Separate Beginnings?*). But there is still widespread acceptance, on the part of both teachers and pupils, that patterns of interaction where boys are more involved than girls are natural. Joan Swann and David Graddol's description of this orientation in relation to primary age children could apply equally to the secondary classroom:

What we observe in the classroom is a consensus . . . where an unequal distribution of talk is seen as normal. In particular, girls seem to have learnt to expect a lower participation level than boys, and boys seem to have learned that their fair share is a larger one. These are expectations which are brought to school by all participants, since such inequalities in the distribution of talk are commonplace amongst adults.

J. Swann and D. Graddol, 'Gender Inequalities in Classroom Talk',
pp. 63–4

And where science in particular is concerned, the misconceptions about the respective abilities of boys and girls abound, with profound implications for subject choice and subsequent career patterns.

Subject options

Until the National Curriculum was introduced under the 1988 Education Reform Act, pupils were allowed a degree of choice in selecting the subjects they studied at secondary school which was considered by many educationalists to be shortsighted. In some schools, children were able to drop subjects in the second year, meaning that they had no education in, say, history or geography or physics after the age of 13. This meant that some children were specialising far too early and, by making particular choices at an age when they were too young to know the full implications of their decisions, were foreclosing on their options at 16 and beyond.

In the case of girls, certain areas including technical and craft subjects (with the exception of domestic science) were widely perceived to be 'off limits'. As a result, as Gillian Blunden, points out ('Vocational Education for Women's Work in England and Wales'), girls were not qualified 'even to apply for many further education courses'. Other subjects were abandoned at the earliest possible opportunity. And these included physics, and, to a lesser degree, chemistry, again with far-reaching occupational implications. While the situation has improved considerably over the past twenty years, girls are still underrepresented in areas such as the natural sciences (with the exception of biology), in design and technology, and in computer studies. When given the choice, they tend to opt for the arts, humanities and social studies.

Under the National Curriculum, children will still be able to exercise choice over the subjects they wish to study for GCSE and A level, but they will *have* to study the three core and seven foundation subjects between the ages of 5 and 16. This will mean that both girls and boys receive a more balanced programme of education than in the past, and that girls cannot give up on the technical and scientific side.

But simply making children study the full range of subjects will not do away with the central problems of motivation and lack of confidence. Schools have to be aware of these issues, and to take steps to surmount them. When choosing a school for a daughter, or supporting a daughter as she progresses

Table 5.1 Females as a percentage of CSE Grade 1 and GCE O- and A-level passes, selected subjects (summer examinations), England and Wales, 1985.

Subject	CSE	O level	A level
Technical drawing	6.23	6.23	3.32
Physics	23.23	28.46	21.34
Computer studies/science	31.80	26.93	15.72
Chemistry	42.74	41.29	36.96
Mathematics	48.68	44.13	–
Mathematics (pure and applied)	–	–	31.58
History	56.68	50.77	51.88
Commerce	62.30	–	–
Commercial subjects	–	57.10	–
Biology	64.65	60.22	60.09
English	60.65	–	70.86
English language	–	56.74	–
English literature	–	60.81	–
Social studies	68.74	–	–
French	69.05	60.96	72.81
German	70.76	62.70	71.07
Sociology	–	74.99	74.26
Business and office practice	90.35	–	–
Domestic subjects	95.71	–	98.90
Cookery	–	96.64	–
All subjects	55.39	51.41	46.21

From: Equal Opportunities Commission, *Women and Men in Britain: a statistical profile* (HMSO, 1987).
Original source: Department of Education and Science and Welsh Joint Education Committee.

toward public exams, I would suggest that it is crucial to talk to the staff responsible for traditionally masculine subjects and to make an assessment of their attitudes towards the girls in their charge. This is a difficult task because, nowadays, nearly all teachers will pay at least lip-service to the provision of equal opportunities, although their lessons and relationship with pupils may tell a different story.

Again, it may be a case of using tact and discretion to test the waters, and then seeing what happens. Parents should not,

I feel, expect staff to work miracles – the silk purse out of a sow's ear syndrome – and nor should they be so concerned about possible sexism that they see it in every comment or omission. But there should be the feeling that girls are *expected* to do well in maths (and that if they are having difficulties, someone will take the trouble to find out why), that they are welcome in the lab or workshop; that, in a way, their presence there is taken for granted rather than seen (and remarked upon) as out of the ordinary. As a parent, I would certainly take issue with the school in my own city where a science teacher told the father of a twelve-year-old girl not to worry about his daughter's difficulties with science: 'We don't really expect the girls to do well in this area'.

One of the aims of education must be to widen children's horizons, so as to provide them with a broad range of possibilities as they move up the school, and in their later lives. This is not done by acceding to their immature judgements as to the subjects they wish to study, and confirming their prejudices either through active agreement, or passive acceptance. I believe that as the National Curriculum is phased in, and as younger teachers come out of their training courses with some awareness of sex as a variable in educational achievement, then the situation will improve. In the meantime, parents would be well advised to inquire into a school's track record: to discover how many girls are opting for the sciences, for technology, for computer studies, to find out how well they are doing in mathematics, and to form their judgements accordingly.

Single-sex or co-educational?

Readers may have gathered from what has gone before that I feel, despite the efforts of many schools to provide a good, all-round education for their female as well as their male pupils, that all in the co-educational garden is not lovely. This is despite the steady improvement in the examination results of girls in recent years (see Figure 5.1), and, indeed, despite the fact that girls are now outstripping boys in terms of the num-

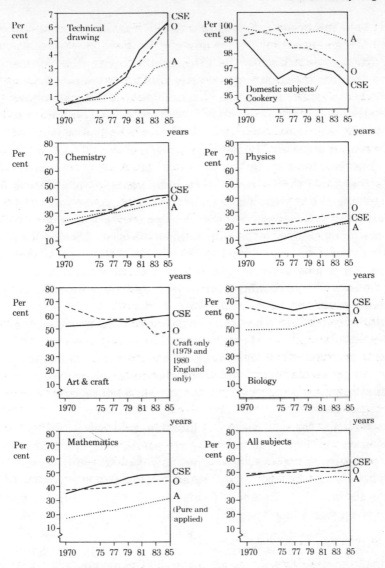

Figure 5.1 Females as a percentage of CSE (grade 1), GCE O- and A-level passes in selected subjects: summer examinations, England and Wales, 1970–85

Source: Department of Education and Science and Welsh Joint Education Committee. Reproduced from: Equal Opportunities Commission, *Women and Men in Britain: a statistical profile*, with the permission of the Controller of Her Majesty's Stationery Office.

73

bers of examinations passed (see *Social Trends* 20, 1990 edition). I hold this view for a number of reasons.

Chief among these is the intractability and, perhaps, the inevitability of sexually conservative attitudes towards female pupils (and staff) among significant subsets of the male school population (see, for example, A. Furnham and B. Gunter, 'Adolescents' Attitudes to the Role of Women'), and on the part of some staff also (see M. Stanworth, *Gender and Schooling*; R. G. Burgess, 'Something You Learn to Live with?'). It seems to me inevitable that during the teenage years, girls and boys are going to be hyperaware of their and their peers' sexuality. Responses to this stage in their development vary enormously: some young people retire into their shell, some become loud and conspicuous, some seem to take it all in their stride. But however a girl responds, she is likely to encounter at least some boys who, in coming to terms with their own masculinity, treat her with what amounts to a profound lack of respect. And it is where this occurs on a day-to-day basis within the context of a school, and combines with peer group pressure to conform, popular cultural images of masculinity and femininity, and the dynamics of mixed-sex classroom interaction that I feel continuing concern for the social and educational well-being of girls.

I feel this concern because education, as I see it, fulfils a social as well as an educational purpose. As well as transmitting culturally approved bodies of knowledge to young people, a purpose which is explicitly stated in official school curriculum documents, schools seek to prepare pupils for adult life in the society to which they belong. This second purpose, while sounding eminently reasonable as a proposition, is less explicitly stated, and its practical meanings and implications are seldom discussed in any great detail outside training colleges and university departments of education. Some educationalists have likened it to a hidden curriculum of knowledge, and it is adequately described by Eileen Byrne as follows:

(the hidden curriculum) transmits to young people a collection of messages about the status and character of individuals and social groups. It works through school organisation, through attitudes, and through omission – what we do not teach, highlight or illuminate, is often more influential as a factor for bias than what we do.

E. Byrne, *Women and Education*, p. 110.

It is in this, albeit amorphous, area of organisation, attitudes and omissions that I believe co-education may do girls a dis-service; that the experience of schooling may lead girls to perceive themselves, and boys to perceive them as somehow less *significant* than boys. It is a message which is very often transmitted, not through explicit statements on the part of either staff or pupils that boys are more important and girls must be content with second place, but through a tacit accept-ance, and hence endorsement, of the sexual status quo. Quite often, perhaps most of the time, it happens with no ill intent. Teachers are so preoccupied with getting through lessons, keeping the attention of their pupils, covering the syllabus, and so on, that there is simply no time to bring out and encourage reticent pupils, and imbue them with a strong sense of self-worth. And so it is that the sexually-related attitudes and assumptions that girls and boys bring with them to the classroom are subtly reinforced, and their manifestation in self-concept and behaviour become more pronounced as chil-dren reach secondary school age (see J. Block, *Sex Role Identity and Ego Development*).

This, then, is how I understand a range of studies which show girls consistently to underrate their abilities in subjects such as the natural sciences (see A. Kelly, 'Girls into Science and Technology'), and in respect of their general intelligence (see L. Higgins, 'The Unknowing of Intelligence'). It goes some way to explaining why female students at Oxford University have been less well represented in the category of students gaining first-class degrees since particular colleges became mixed rather than single-sex (see J. Hart, B. Davies and R. Harré, *Oxford Review of Education*, 1990). And it explains, at least in part, why comparatively few women are involved in the talk-based decision-making bodies such as the Trades Union Movement, professional organisations, local and national government, which affect all of our lives (see Equal Opportunities Commission, *Women and Men in Britain*).

Despite my misgivings, however, I readily admit to the fact that it is extremely difficult to weigh up the respective advantages and disadvantages of single-sex and co-educational secondary schools in purely educational terms (see A. Bone, *Girls and Girls-Only Schools*; and R. Deem [ed.] *Schooling for Women's Work*). This is because a number of factors other than pupil sex have to be taken into account. We know, for example, that the socio-economic backgrounds of pupils are very strongly implicated in how well or badly they are likely to do at school. We know also that the influence of the individual headteacher and his or her staff in determining the ethos of a school can be crucial. And that the peer group can and does influence some children, adversely or otherwise. The combination of these and other factors can mean that a good co-educational secondary school with a strong head and an atmosphere in which girls are valued could be a better bet than a girls' school without these attributes. The parent facing up to this particular, complex choice is not, it has to be said, in for an easy time!

The independent sector

Although only just over 7 per cent of all children are educated within the independent sector, the number of parents choosing this form of education for their daughters has increased significantly in recent years. This may be due partly to increased levels of affluence among certain sections of the population. But it may also have occurred in response to comprehensive reorganisation, which, in many instances has led to single-sex grammar or direct grant schools either becoming independent, or amalgamating as co-educational comprehensives. Parents who wish to provide their daughters with a single-sex and/or a selective education are therefore finding that these options are, increasingly, available only within the independent sector.

Every parent considering using the independent sector should be fully aware that 'private' does not automatically mean 'better'. There are some poor independent schools just as there are some poor maintained schools, and parents are well advised to consult specialist organisations such as the Independent Schools Information Service (ISIS) before any major decisions are made. And as with any school, parents should visit, talk to as many people involved with the school as possible, read the school's prospectus, consider its results, and try to gauge its atmosphere.

There is no doubt that some of the established girls' schools obtain excellent academic results, and have a strong record in encouraging their pupils to enter non-traditional areas. If you do consider the single-sex option, this question is worth bearing in mind. Looking back over the research evidence on the achievements of girls in both the single-sex and the co-educational sector, it is possible to distinguish two types of girls' school. One is the type which tended to envisage its girls going to finishing school rather than to university or college, and making a 'good match'. In such schools, facilities for studying the sciences and technology were limited, and girls were in fact more likely to encounter and to opt for these subjects within the context of a good co-educational school. The second type always had its sights set on higher education and careers, and provided opportunities in non-traditional as well as traditional subject areas. Girls attending this type of school were always more likely (because of factors such as selective entry and excellent teacher–pupil ratios as well as the single-sex dimension) than girls in co-educational schools to opt for subjects such as physics and chemistry.

Recent trends and developments have meant that both types of school have had to adapt, so that their existence as types is no longer so easily discernible. It is still important, however, to investigate whether facilities are available for girls to study, say, design and technology (which all pupils in maintained schools will study under the National Curriculum), to check the extent of their facilities, and to establish whether the school employs the specialist staff to teach these subjects.

Boys' schools and the move to co-education

Parents who wish to consider the independent sector should also look into the growing number of boys' schools which, over the past twenty years, have either admitted girls into their sixth forms, or have become completely co-educational. The trend towards co-education reflects a demand on the part of parents, the prevailing pattern within the maintained sector, and competition between schools for pupils – and looks set to continue.

Again, parents should look into the case of each individual school under consideration, and make an assessment as to how it would suit their daughter. There is little point, for example, in sending a shy, self-conscious 13-year-old girl to what is still to all intents and purposes a boys' school, where girls have to learn to be 'one of the chaps'. Where girls have obviously been brought in as an afterthought, to boost falling rolls, or because such-and-such a school down the road did it, the advice must be to steer well clear.

There is no doubt, however, that some schools have made great efforts to adapt to the presence of girls, and that some girls work better in the company of boys. Again, efforts must be made to match the character of the individual child with the character of the school. But whereas a maintained school is obliged to make provision for all-comers, independent schools may select in terms of both ability and character. This does have the advantage of making the parents' task in choosing a school easier: they can see for themselves whether the school's (usually clear) ethos and atmosphere will suit their child.

The 'cloister' effect

Some parents are put off single-sex schools, whether in the maintained or the independent sector, because they fear that it is unnatural for the sexes to be so much apart, and that this separation may lead to difficulties in girls and boys being able to relate to one another as normal individuals outside school and in adult life. This is a reasonable enough fear. Yet as somebody who went to a girls' school, and who continues to believe that the single-sex option should be kept open, there are several points to be made in its defence. The first is that a great many single-sex schools now ensure that their pupils mix with the other sex within the context of drama or music groups, outdoor pursuits, discussion groups and school societies, and leisure activities such as discos, theatre trips and so on. Secondly, parents bear some responsibility to ensure that their children mix outside school. And finally, what passes for normal interaction between the sexes within school may in fact be interaction in which, as we have seen, girls are routinely marginalised. The experience of normal interaction may account at least in part for the fact that:

- children attending co-educational schools were found by Her Majesty's Inspectorate to be more likely to opt for traditional girls'/boys' subjects than children attending single-sex schools (DES, 1975)

- single-sex teaching can lead to dramatic improvements in girls' performance in both maths (S. Smith, *Separate Tables?* and *Separate Beginnings?*), and science (J. Harding, 'Sex Differences in Performance in Science Examinations').

- female social mobility has been greater amongst those educated in the single-sex, ex-grammar sector (J. Shaw, 'The Politics of Single-sex Schools'; and see also A. Heath, *Social Mobility*).

Girls in the co-educational sector

The fact remains, however, that the vast majority of British secondary school children are educated in co-educational comprehensive schools. And parents should not be made to feel that this form of education is somehow second-best. Girls *can* and *do* achieve excellent results.

Those of us involved in education, whether as teachers or parents, have a responsibility to ensure that the encouraging trends seen over recent years continue; that girls as well as boys get a fair deal. In most schools, there is an evident commitment to this ideal: some teachers will have covered issues of gender and education in pre- and/or in-service training, and there should be a general awareness of the problems girls may face. As a result, staff may take trouble to ensure that girls are included in lessons, that excessive dominance by boys is not allowed to happen, and that girls as well as boys receive liberal rather than narrowly traditional careers advice. I also sense, although I must admit to having no impressive sets of figures to lend weight to my observation, that girls themselves are increasingly aware of gender-related issues – and increasingly unwilling to remain forever in the shade.

This tendency, together with the increased involvement of parents in education, and the more balanced approach in prospect with the National Curriculum must give all those concerned with the education of girls a good measure of hope for the future.

Chapter 6

CONCLUSION

In this book, I have tried to cover a range of issues concerning the education of girls. Some of these issues were of a general nature, and will be already familiar to many parents. Others were very much more particular in focus, and may have introduced some readers to the less obvious differences in both the behaviour of girls and boys, and the response of adults to them. Both sorts of issue are important. For it is no good paying lip-service to the idea of fair play, and of providing girls with opportunities to extend their horizons if, at the same time, our everyday practices and ways of relating to girls carry a less encouraging and confidence-enhancing message. This is effectively to hold out an opportunity with one hand, and hang on to it with the other.

Obviously, I have not been able to cover every possible angle on the question of girls and their education. I am especially conscious that I have not touched upon race, and how it may work in conjunction with factors such as religion and sex. I feel, rightly or wrongly, that issues such as the establishment of separate Muslim girls' schools call for detailed discussion of fundamental questions concerning our conceptions of sexuality, and the nature and purposes of education. These questions deserve their own book.

I am also aware that books about education tend to appeal to a particular type of parent; that as an author, you stand a more than odds-on chance of finding yourself preaching to the already converted! This is perhaps especially so in the case of girls. For the remarkable strides made by girls over the past twenty years in catching up with their brothers, have nearly all been made by middle-class girls. The sort of girls who, 20, 30, 40 years ago, would have been content to play a nicely modulated second fiddle to a male boss, but who now want to call the tune. At the same time, for most working-class girls, from the lower bands and streams of our secondary schools, who go on to work in shops, factories and offices, very little has changed. This should come as a salutary lesson to those commentators who are so fond of telling us that we now live in a 'post-feminist' age.

Education alone, however 'girl-friendly', will not substantially change the lives of these girls and women, but it can help. And parents who care about and become involved in their children's schools can do much to bring issues to the attention of other parents and of teachers. By doing this, they stand to help other people's children as well as their own.

Finally, and on a more individual level, it has to be said that buying your daughter a Lego set, letting her swing from the trees and get dirty, making her so assertive that her very appearance causes the boys to shrink away from the computer, will not guarantee her the Nobel Prize for Physics. Daughters have minds of their own, and there comes a time when over-pushy parents get short shrift. We have to remember that not everyone, male or female, wants to be counted in the ranks of the Great Achievers, nor do all women want to join in the, at times, dubious pleasures of combining career and motherhood. Education represents very much more than a qualification to jockey for position in the rat-race, and we have to maintain a balance between quality of life and the ambition to succeed. As parents and as teachers, we can only do our best to remove the unnecessary obstacles, to make the conditions as fair as possible, and to help our daughters anticipate the consequences of their actions and choices.

REFERENCES AND FURTHER READING

S. Acker, 'Women and Teaching: a semi-detached sociology of a semi-profession' in S. Walker and L. Barton (eds) *Gender, Class and Education* (Falmer, Lewes, 1983).

S. Acker, J. Megarry, S. Nisbet and E. Hoyle (eds) *World Yearbook of Education 1984: Women and Education* (Kogan Page, London, 1984).

J. Block, *Sex Role Identity and Ego Development* (Jossey Bass, San Francisco, 1985).

G. Blunden, 'Vocational Education for Women's Work in England and Wales' in S. Acker, J. Megarry, S. Nisbet and E. Hoyle (eds) *World Yearbook of Education 1984: Women and Education* (Kogan Page, London, 1984).

A. Bone, *Girls and Girls-Only Schools: a review of the evidence* (Equal Opportunities Commission, Manchester, 1983).

R. G. Burgess, 'Something You Learn to Live with? Gender and inequality in a comprehensive school', *Gender and Education*, vol. 1, no. 2 (1989).

L. Burton, *Girls into Maths Can Go* (Holt Education, London, 1986).

E. Byrne, *Women and Education* (Tavistock, London, 1978).

K. Clarricoates, 'Dinosaurs in the Classroom: a re-examination of some aspects of the hidden curriculum in primary schools', *Women's Studies International Quarterly*, vol. 1, no. 4 (1978), pp. 353–64.

P. Croll, 'Teacher Interaction with Individual Male and Female Pupils in Junior Age Classrooms', *Educational Research*, vol. 26, no. 2 (1985).

R. R. Dale, *Mixed or Single-Sex School?*, vols 1–3 (Routledge and Kegan Paul, London; 1969, 1971, 1974).

B. C. Dart and J. A. Clarke, 'Sexism in Schools: a new look', *Educational Review*, vol. 40, no. 1 (1988).

R. Deem (ed.) *Schooling for Women's Work* (Routledge and Kegan Paul, London, 1980).

R. Deem (ed.) *Co-Education Re-Considered* (Open University Press, Milton Keynes, 1984).

S. Delamont, *Sex Roles and the School* (Methuen, London, 1980).

E. G. Doherty and C. Culver, 'Sex-role Identification, Ability and Achievement among High School Girls', *Sociology of Education*, vol. 43 (1976).

K. Durkin, *Television, Sex Roles and Children* (Open University Press, Milton Keynes, 1985).

C. A. Dwyer, 'Sex Differences in Reading: an evaluation and a critique of current methods', *Review of Educational Research*, vol. 43 (1973).

Equal Opportunities Commission, *Women and Men in Britain: a statistical profile* (HMSO, 1987).

D. Freeman, *Margaret Mead and Samoa: the making and unmaking of an anthropological myth* (Harvard University Press, Cambridge, Massachusetts, 1983).

J. French, 'Gender and the Classroom', *New Society* (7 March 1986).

J. French and P. French, 'Gender Imbalances in the Primary Classroom: an interactional account', *Educational Research*, vol. 26, no. 2 (1984).

J. French and P. French, *Gender Imbalances in Infant School Classroom Interaction: Final Report to the Equal Opportunities Commission* (The College of Ripon and York St John, Lord Mayor's Walk, York, 1986).

A. Furnham and B. Gunter, 'Adolescents' Attitudes to the Role of Women', *Educational Studies*, vol. 14, no. 2 (1988).

M. Grabrucker, *There's a Good Girl: gender stereotyping in the first three years of life: a diary* (The Women's Press, London, 1988).

B. Gunter, *Television and Sex Role Stereotyping* (John Libbey, London, 1986).

J. Harding, 'Sex Differences in Performance in Science Examinations' in R. Deem (ed.) *Schooling for Women's Work* (Routledge and Kegan Paul, London, 1980).

J. Hart, B. Davies and R. Harré, *Oxford Review of Education*, vol. 15, no. 3 (1990).

T. J. Harvey, 'Science in Single-sex and Mixed Teaching Groups', *Educational Research*, vol. 27, no. 3 (1985).

A. Heath, *Social Mobility* (Fontana, London, 1981).

L. Higgins, 'The Unknowing of Intelligence', *The Guardian* (10 February 1987).

J. Hodgeon, *A Woman's World: report on a project in Cleveland nurseries on sex differentiation in the early years* (Cleveland Education Committee, 1985).

C. N. Jacklin, 'Boys and Girls Entering School' in M. Marland (ed.) *Sex Differentiation and Schooling* (Heinemann, London, 1983).

J. Kamm, *How Different From Us: a biography of Miss Buss and Miss Beale* (Bodley Head, London, 1958).

A. Kelly (ed.) *The Missing Half: girls and science education* (Manchester University Press, Manchester, 1981).

A. Kelly, *Final Report from the Girls into Science and Technology Project to the Joint Panel on Women and Underachievement of the Equal Opportunities Commission and the Social Science Research Council* (Girls into Science and Technology, Manchester, 1984).

G. Lobban, 'Sex Roles in Reading Schemes', *Educational Review*, vol. 27, no. 3 (1975).

E. E. Maccoby and C. N. Jacklin, *The Psychology of Sex Differences* (Stanford University Press, Stanford, California, 1975).

P. Mahony, *Schools for the Boys? Co-education re-assessed* (Hutchinson, London, 1985).

M. Marland (ed.) *Sex Differentiation and Schooling* (Heinemann, London, 1983).

M. Mead, *Male and Female* (Pelican, London, 1949).

M. Messenger Davies, *Television is Good for your Kids* (Hilary Shipman, London, 1989).

V. Morgan and S. Dunn, 'Chameleons in the Classroom: visible and invisible children in nursery and infant classrooms', *Educational Review*, vol. 40, no. 1 (1988).

A. Oakley, *Sex, Gender and Society* (Temple Smith, 1975).

Schools' Inquiry Commission (Report of the Commissioners, 1868).

L. A. Serbin, 'The Hidden Curriculum: academic consequences of teacher expectations' in M. Marland (ed.) *Sex Differentiation and Schooling* (Heinemann, London, 1983).

J. Shaw, 'The Politics of Single-sex Schools' in R. Deem (ed.) *Schooling for Women's Work* (Routledge and Kegan Paul, London, 1980).

C. Smith and B. Lloyd, 'Maternal Behaviour and Perceived Sex of Infant: revisited', *Child Development*, vol. 49 (1978).

S. Smith, *Separate Tables? An investigation into single-sex setting in mathematics* (Equal Opportunities Commission, Manchester, 1986).

S. Smith, *Separate Beginnings? (A supplementary study to Separate Tables?)* (Equal Opportunities Commission, Manchester, 1987).

Social Trends 20 (HMSO, 1990).

I. Sonesson (1989) *Who Brings Up Our Children – the Video or We Ourselves?* (Solna, Sweden: Esselte Studium).

M. Stanworth, *Gender and Schooling: a study of sexual divisions in the classroom* (Hutchinson, in association with the Explorations in Feminism Collective, 1983).

J. Swann and D. Graddol, 'Gender Inequalities in Classroom Talk', *English in Education*, vol. 22, no. 1 (1988).

R. Walden and V. Walkerdine, *Girls and Mathematics: the early years* (University of London Institute of Education, Bedford Way Papers no. 8, 1982).

L. R. Walum, *The Dynamics of Sex and Gender* (Rand McNally, New York, 1977).

J. Whyte, *Girls into Science and Technology: the story of a project* (Routledge and Kegan Paul, Henley, 1986).

INDEX